Better Homes and Gardens®

fresh and simple™

pasta
pronto

Better Homes and Gardens® Books

Des Moines, Iowa

All of us at Better Homes and Gardens® Books are dedicated to providing you with the information and ideas you need to create delicious foods. We welcome your comments and suggestions. Write to us at Better Homes and Gardens® Books, Cookbook Editorial Department, RW-240, 1716 Locust St., Des Moines, IA 50309-3023.

If you would like to order additional copies of any of our books, check with your local bookstore.

Our seal assures you that every recipe in *Pasta Pronto* has been tested in the Better Homes and Gardens® Test Kitchen. This means that each recipe is practical and reliable, and meets our high standards of taste appeal. We guarantee your satisfaction with this book for as long as you own it.

Pictured on front cover: Rigatoni With Eggplant & Dried Tomato Pesto (see recipe, *page 28*)
Pictured on page 1: Penne with Broccoli & Dried Tomatoes (see recipe, *page 31*)

Better Homes and Gardens® Books
An imprint of Meredith® Books

Fresh and Simple™ *Pasta Pronto*
Editor: Jennifer Darling
Contributing Editors: Connie Hay, Marla Mason
Writer: Jane Horn
Designer: Craig Hanken
Copy Editor: Jennifer Speer Ramundt
Proofreader: Mary Pas
Electronic Production Coordinator: Paula Forest
Editorial and Design Assistants: Judy Bailey, Jennifer Norris, Karen Schirm
Test Kitchen Director: Sharon Stilwell
Test Kitchen Product Supervisor: Marilyn Cornelius
Food Stylists: Susan Draudt, Dianna Nolin, Janet Pittman
Photographers: Jim Krantz, Kritsada Panichgul
Prop Stylist: Nancy Wall Hopkins
Production Director: Douglas M. Johnston
Production Manager: Pam Kvitne
Assistant Prepress Manager: Marjorie J. Schenkelberg

Meredith® Books
Editor in Chief: James D. Blume
Design Director: Matt Strelecki
Managing Editor: Gregory H. Kayko
Executive Food Editor: Lisa Holderness

Director, Sales & Marketing, Retail: Michael A. Peterson
Director, Sales & Marketing, Special Markets: Rita McMullen
Director, Sales & Marketing, Home & Garden Center Channel: Ray Wolf
Director, Operations: Valerie Wiese

Vice President, General Manager: Jamie L. Martin

Better Homes and Gardens® Magazine
Editor in Chief: Jean LemMon
Executive Food Editor: Nancy Byal

Meredith Publishing Group
President, Publishing Group: Christopher M. Little
Vice President, Consumer Marketing & Development: Hal Oringer

Meredith Corporation
Chairman and Chief Executive Officer: William T. Kerr

Chairman of the Executive Committee: E. T. Meredith III

contents

great tasting
meals in no time flat

Stop watching the clock! Here are 66 simple, delicious dinners that assemble in a flash no matter how busy your day. The flavors are global, the ingredients everyday, the tastes altogether fresh and new. They make cooking fun again.

Ever-popular pasta is the star, smoothly switching roles from salads to soups to international classics with flair but not fuss. It proves the perfect partner to any food or any occasion, weekday through weekend. If you crave a shortcut to good eating, *Pasta Pronto* will speed the way.

lots of
pasta

wide noodles with
chicken & lima beans

Any width pasta will do here, but the wider the noodle, the more you get per mouthful of this luscious, creamy sauce. If your pantry yields lasagna noodles, just cook 'em up, then cut them crosswise into 1-inch strips.

Start to finish: 30 minutes   Makes 4 servings

Cook pasta according to package directions, adding lima beans to water with the pasta. Drain pasta and beans; return to saucepan.

Meanwhile, place undrained tomatoes in a food processor or blender container. Cover and process or blend until pureed; set aside.

Rinse chicken; pat dry. Cut chicken into bite-size pieces. For sauce, in a large skillet cook chicken, onion, and pepper in hot oil over medium-high heat for 2 to 3 minutes or until chicken is no longer pink. Reduce heat; stir in tomatoes and chicken broth. Simmer about 5 minutes or until liquid is reduced by half. Stir in cream; simmer for 2 to 3 minutes more or until sauce is desired consistency.

Pour sauce over pasta mixture; toss gently to coat. Transfer pasta mixture to a warm serving dish. If desired, sprinkle with Parmesan cheese and chives.

Nutrition facts per serving: 503 cal., 12 g total fat (4 g sat. fat), 43 mg chol., 438 mg sodium, 75 g carbo., 7 g fiber, 25 g pro. Daily values: 14% vit. A, 21% vit. C, 5% calcium, 34% iron

Note: If you prefer, substitute lasagna noodles for the pappardelle. Cook them according to package directions. Drain and cut crosswise into 1-inch pieces. (If you use frozen lasagna noodles, cook the lima beans separately as they will cook longer than the noodles.)

- 8 ounces dried pappardelle, mafalda, fettuccine, or wide egg noodles*
- 1 10-ounce package frozen baby lima beans
- 1 14½-ounce can Italian-style stewed tomatoes, undrained
- 6 ounces skinless, boneless chicken breast halves
- 1 small onion, cut into wedges
- ¼ teaspoon coarsely ground black pepper
- 1 tablespoon olive oil
- ¼ cup chicken broth
- ¼ cup whipping cream
- Shredded Parmesan cheese (optional)
- Snipped fresh chives (optional)

chicken & pasta primavera

This almost effortless saucepan pasta gets fresh flavor from year-round market staples. A sour cream and mustard combo infused with fresh herbs wraps the meal in a creamy, tangy sauce.

8

- **1** 9-ounce package refrigerated spinach or plain fettuccine
- **2** medium carrots, thinly sliced
- **1** medium zucchini, halved lengthwise and thinly sliced
- **¾** cup frozen whole kernel corn
- **12** ounces deli-roasted chicken, cut into ½-inch strips (about 2½ cups)
- **1½** cups chicken broth
- **4** teaspoons cornstarch
- **1** tablespoon snipped fresh tarragon or basil
- **2** teaspoons finely shredded lemon peel
- **½** cup dairy sour cream
- **2** tablespoons Dijon-style mustard

Start to finish: 25 minutes Makes 6 servings

Cook pasta according to package directions, adding carrots, zucchini, and corn to the water with the pasta. Drain pasta and vegetables. Return all to pan; add chicken. (If chicken has been refrigerated, place it in a colander. Pour pasta, vegetables, and cooking liquid over chicken; drain.)

Meanwhile, in a medium saucepan combine chicken broth, cornstarch, tarragon, and lemon peel. Cook and stir over medium heat until thickened and bubbly. Cook and stir for 1 minute more. Remove from heat; stir in sour cream and mustard. Pour over pasta mixture, tossing to coat. Serve immediately.

Nutrition facts per serving: 321 cal., 9 g total fat (4 g sat. fat), 97 mg chol., 425 mg sodium, 32 g carbo., 1 g fiber, 27 g pro. Daily values: 62% vit. A, 5% vit. C, 6% calcium, 19% iron

chicken & vegetables
with spicy asian sauce

In less time than it takes to order in, you can sit down at home to a delicious Asian-style meal. There's no stir-frying to do or complicated sauces to compose. Just heat, mix, and serve.

Start to finish: 30 minutes   Makes 4 servings

Cook pasta according to package directions. Place the pea pods and chicken in a large colander. Pour pasta and cooking liquid over pea pods and chicken in colander; drain well. Add pineapple. Transfer the pasta mixture to a warm serving dish.

Meanwhile, for sauce, in a small saucepan heat and stir chicken broth and peanut butter until peanut butter melts. Stir in soy sauce, lime juice, red pepper, and garlic; heat through.

To serve, spoon sauce over pasta mixture.

Nutrition facts per serving: 289 cal., 6 g total fat (1 g sat. fat), 34 mg chol., 234 mg sodium, 40 g carbo., 4 g fiber, 20 g pro. Daily values: 7% vit. A, 44% vit. C, 3% calcium, 21% iron

6 **ounces dried tomato fettuccine or linguine**

2 **cups fresh pea pods, tips trimmed, or one 6-ounce package frozen pea pods**

1 **cup chopped cooked chicken or turkey**

1 **cup coarsely chopped fresh pineapple or one 8-ounce can pineapple chunks, drained**

¼ **cup reduced-sodium chicken broth**

1 **tablespoon creamy peanut butter**

1 **tablespoon reduced-sodium soy sauce**

1 **tablespoon lime juice or lemon juice**

⅛ **teaspoon crushed red pepper**

1 **clove garlic, minced**

turkey piccata with fettuccine

Ultraconvenient turkey steaks fully cook in minutes, just long enough to yield the tasty juices and crusty flavor bits that jump-start a snappy pan sauce.

4 ounces dried fettuccine or linguine

¼ cup all-purpose flour

½ teaspoon lemon-pepper seasoning or pepper

4 turkey breast tenderloin steaks (about 1 pound total)

2 tablespoons olive oil or cooking oil

⅓ cup dry white wine

2 tablespoons lemon juice

2 tablespoons water

½ teaspoon instant chicken bouillon granules

1 tablespoon capers, rinsed and drained (optional)

2 tablespoons snipped fresh parsley

Start to finish: 30 minutes   Makes 4 servings

Cook pasta according to package directions; drain.

Meanwhile, in a bowl stir together flour and lemon-pepper seasoning.

Rinse turkey; pat dry. Place between sheets of plastic wrap; pound to ⅛-inch thickness. Dip turkey slices in flour mixture to coat.

In a 12-inch skillet cook turkey steaks in hot oil over medium-high heat about 2 minutes per side or until light golden brown and no longer pink. Remove from pan; cover and keep warm.

For sauce, add wine, lemon juice, water, and bouillon granules to skillet, scraping up crusty bits from bottom of pan. If desired, stir in capers. Bring to boiling. Simmer, uncovered, for 2 minutes. Remove from heat; add parsley.

To serve, divide pasta among 4 plates. Top each with a turkey steak and spoon sauce over all.

Nutrition facts per serving: 331 cal., 10 g total fat (2 g sat. fat), 50 mg chol., 292 mg sodium, 31 g carbo., 0 g fiber, 26 g pro. Daily values: 1% vit. A, 21% vit. C, 2% calcium, 18% iron

shells stuffed with turkey & lentils

If you love the flavors of lasagna, but not its richness, try this stuffed pasta created with today's health-conscious diets in mind. Ground turkey, naturally low-fat lentils, and a lighter, herb-seasoned sauce make the difference.

11

Prep: 30 minutes   Bake: 25 minutes   Makes 5 servings

Cook pasta according to package directions; drain. Meanwhile, for filling, in a large saucepan cook turkey and onion until turkey is no longer pink. Add tomatoes, Italian seasoning, nutmeg, and pepper. Reduce heat and simmer for 5 minutes, stirring often. Stir in lentils. Remove from heat. Stir in ½ cup of the Alfredo sauce, the ricotta cheese, half of the mozzarella cheese, and the parsley. Spoon about 2 tablespoons filling into each pasta shell or about ⅓ cup into each manicotti shell.

Arrange filled pasta shells in a lightly greased 2-quart rectangular baking dish. Bake, covered, in a 375° oven for 15 minutes. Sprinkle with remaining mozzarella cheese and the Parmesan cheese. Bake about 10 minutes more or until cheese is golden brown.

Meanwhile, heat remaining Alfredo sauce; spoon sauce onto plates. Place 3 pasta shells or 2 manicotti on each plate.

Nutrition facts per serving: 474 cal., 19 g total fat (9 g sat. fat), 64 mg chol., 986 mg sodium, 50 g carbo., 3 g fiber, 28 g pro. Daily values: 20% vit. A, 23% vit. C, 29% calcium, 23% iron

To make ahead: Fill pasta shells and arrange in baking dish. Pour remaining sauce over top. Seal, label, and freeze. (Freeze cheese topping separately.) Before cooking, thaw overnight in refrigerator. Bake, covered, in a 350° oven for 55 minutes. Uncover; sprinkle with cheese topping. Bake about 10 minutes more or until cheese is golden and pasta is heated through.

- 15 dried jumbo pasta shells or 10 manicotti shells
- ½ pound ground raw turkey
- 1 small onion, finely chopped
- 3 large plum tomatoes, seeded and finely chopped
- 1 tablespoon Italian seasoning, crushed
- ½ teaspoon ground nutmeg
- ¼ teaspoon pepper
- 1 cup canned lentils, rinsed and drained, or cooked lentils
- 1 15-ounce container refrigerated light Alfredo sauce (about 2 cups)
- ½ cup nonfat ricotta cheese or cream-style cottage cheese
- ½ cup shredded reduced-fat mozzarella cheese
- ¼ cup snipped fresh parsley
- ¼ cup grated Parmesan cheese

summer pasta with pork

This colorful dish marries all the elements of a delicious warm-weather dinner. Fresh-from-the-garden green beans and summer squash, combined with a few pantry foods like dried mushrooms and tomatoes, means dinner al fresco is a few easy steps away.

Start to finish: 30 minutes   Makes 4 servings

Soak mushrooms and tomatoes for 5 minutes in enough boiling water to cover. Drain and snip, discarding mushroom stems; set aside.

Cook pasta according to package directions, adding beans to the water with pasta. Add squash the last 2 minutes of cooking. Drain; keep warm.

Meanwhile, stir together the milk, chicken broth, onion, cornstarch, lemon-pepper seasoning, and salt; set aside. Season pork lightly with additional salt and lemon-pepper seasoning. In a medium skillet cook pork in hot oil over medium heat for 5 to 6 minutes per side or until juices run clear and only a little pink remains in center of meat. Remove meat from skillet; cut into thin, bite-size strips. Keep warm.

For sauce, drain fat from skillet. Pour cornstarch mixture into skillet. Cook and stir until thickened and bubbly, scraping up any brown bits from bottom of skillet. Reduce heat; cook for 2 minutes more. Stir in mushrooms and tomatoes.

Divide pasta mixture among 4 plates. Arrange pork on each plate; spoon sauce over all.

Nutrition facts per serving: 453 cal., 20 g total fat (8 g sat. fat), 110 mg chol., 659 mg sodium, 43 g carbo., 2 g fiber, 26 g pro. Daily values: 14% vit. A, 16% vit. C, 23% iron

- 2 tablespoons dried mushrooms such as shiitake or porcini
- ¼ cup dried tomatoes (not oil packed)
- 6 ounces dried trenne or bow ties
- 2 cups green beans cut into 1-inch pieces
- 1 medium yellow summer squash, sliced (1¼ cups)
- 1 cup milk
- ¾ cup chicken broth
- 1 green onion, sliced
- 1 tablespoon cornstarch
- ½ teaspoon lemon-pepper seasoning
- ¼ teaspoon salt
- 1 pound boneless pork loin chops, cut about ¾ to 1 inch thick
- 1 tablespoon olive oil

thai pork & vegetable curry

Give a traditional Thai curry a new, cross-cultural spin by serving it over Italian orzo pasta instead of the usual rice. Prepared curry paste adds authentic flavor without fuss.

14

1⅓	cups orzo
2	tablespoons cooking oil
12	ounces pork tenderloin or lean boneless pork, cut into bite-size pieces
8	ounces green beans, bias-sliced into 1½-inch pieces (2 cups)*
1	red sweet pepper, cut into thin bite-size strips
2	green onions, bias-sliced into ¼-inch pieces
1	14-ounce can reduced-fat unsweetened coconut milk
4	teaspoons bottled curry paste
2	teaspoons sugar
2	tablespoons lime juice

Start to finish: 30 minutes Makes 4 servings

Cook orzo according to package directions; drain.

Pour 1 tablespoon oil into a large nonstick skillet. Preheat over medium-high heat. Add pork; stir-fry about 4 minutes or until no pink remains. Remove from skillet.

Add remaining 1 tablespoon oil to skillet. Add green beans; stir-fry for 3 minutes. Add sweet pepper and green onions; stir-fry about 2 minutes more or until vegetables are crisp-tender. Add coconut milk, curry paste, and sugar. Reduce heat to low, stirring until combined. Stir in cooked pork and lime juice; heat through. Serve immediately over orzo.

Nutrition facts per serving: 489 cal., 18 g total fat (6 g sat. fat), 60 mg chol., 79 mg sodium, 55 g carbo., 1 g fiber, 27 g pro. Daily values: 18% vit. A, 65% vit. C, 3% calcium, 31% iron

*Note: A 9-ounce package of frozen cut green beans, thawed, may be substituted for the fresh beans. Add them to the skillet with the sweet pepper and onions; stir-fry as directed.

the **thai** pantry
Along with Asian markets, many groceries now stock coconut milk and curry paste, two classic Thai ingredients. Sold in cans in regular and reduced-fat versions, coconut milk is a creamy blend of fresh coconut meat and water. Bottled curry paste blends herbs, spices, and fiery chilies.

spaghetti alla carbonara

If this lighter version of a trattoria classic sounds like bacon and eggs Italian-style, you may be right. Some say America's favorite breakfast duo inspired the classic Roman favorite, traditionally made with cream.

Start to finish: 30 minutes **Makes 4 servings**

Cook pasta according to package directions; drain.

Meanwhile, spray a medium saucepan with nonstick coating. Cook bacon in saucepan until crisp. Drain on paper towels. Wipe saucepan clean with a paper towel.

For sauce, in the same saucepan combine egg, milk, peas, sweet pepper, salt, and crushed red pepper. Cook and stir over medium heat about 6 minutes or just until the mixture coats a metal spoon. Do not boil. Stir in bacon and half of the Parmesan cheese; heat through.

Immediately pour sauce over pasta; toss to coat. Transfer to a warm serving dish. Sprinkle with remaining Parmesan cheese and black pepper.

Nutrition facts per serving: 361 cal., 9 g total fat (2 g sat. fat), 72 mg chol., 326 mg sodium, 52 g carbo., 1 g fiber, 19 g pro. Daily values: 14% vit. A, 20% vit. C, 18% calcium, 18% iron

8 ounces dried spaghetti or linguine

Nonstick spray coating

2 slices turkey bacon, cut crosswise into 1-inch pieces

1 beaten egg

1 cup milk

½ cup frozen peas

¼ cup chopped red sweet pepper

¼ teaspoon salt

¼ teaspoon crushed red pepper

½ cup freshly shredded or grated Parmesan cheese (2 ounces)

Freshly ground black pepper

bow ties with sausage & sweet peppers

You will be amazed that so few ingredients generate so much flavor. For a lower-fat version, use Italian-style ground turkey sausage.

8 **ounces dried large bow ties**

¾ **pound spicy Italian sausage links**

2 **medium red sweet peppers, cut into ¾-inch pieces**

½ **cup vegetable broth or beef broth**

¼ **teaspoon coarsely ground black pepper**

¼ **cup snipped fresh Italian parsley**

Start to finish: 25 minutes   Makes 4 servings

Cook pasta according to package directions; drain. Return pasta to saucepan.

Meanwhile, cut the sausage into 1-inch pieces. In a large skillet cook sausage and sweet peppers over medium-high heat until sausage is brown. Drain off fat.

Stir the broth and black pepper into skillet. Bring to boiling. Reduce heat and simmer, uncovered, for 5 minutes. Remove from heat. Pour over pasta; add parsley. Toss gently to coat. Transfer to a warm serving dish.

Nutrition facts per serving: 397 cal., 18 g total fat (6 g sat. fat), 94 mg chol., 713 mg sodium, 38 g carbo., 3 g fiber, 24 g pro. Daily values: 31% vit. A, 114% vit. C, 4% calcium, 19% iron

mediterranean mostaccioli

The sun-kissed flavors of the Mediterranean shine through in a piquant meat sauce just right for tubular mostaccioli. The mix of chunky vegetables, fresh basil, feta cheese, and ground lamb is country cooking at its simple best.

6 **ounces dried mostaccioli or gemelli**

½ **of a medium eggplant, cubed (about 3 cups)**

2 **cups sliced zucchini**

8 **ounces ground lamb or ground beef**

2 **14- to 15-ounce cans diced tomatoes with olive oil, garlic, and spices or diced tomatoes with garlic and herbs, undrained**

½ **cup raisins**

¼ **cup snipped fresh basil**

½ **teaspoon ground cinnamon**

2 **tablespoons balsamic vinegar**

½ **cup crumbled feta cheese (optional)**

Start to finish: 30 minutes   Makes 4 servings

Cook pasta according to package directions, adding eggplant and zucchini the last 2 minutes of cooking. Drain; keep warm.

Meanwhile, for sauce, in a large skillet cook meat until brown; drain. Stir in undrained tomatoes, raisins, basil, and cinnamon. Bring to boiling. Reduce heat and simmer, covered, for 5 minutes, stirring once or twice. Remove from heat; stir in vinegar.

Transfer pasta mixture to a warm serving platter. Spoon sauce over pasta mixture. If desired, sprinkle with feta cheese.

Nutrition facts per serving: 432 cal., 8 g total fat (3 g sat. fat), 38 mg chol., 939 mg sodium, 72 g carbo., 7 g fiber, 18 g pro. Daily values: 14% vit. A, 48% vit. C, 5% calcium, 25% iron

southwestern wagon wheels

Commercial chili powder is likely a Texas invention of the late 1800s. A welcome convenience, it was an instant hit for the way it delivered in just a few shakes an authentic chili taste to hearty suppers like this one.

Start to finish: 30 minutes   Makes 4 servings

Cook pasta according to package directions, adding broccoli and corn the last 5 minutes of cooking; drain. Return pasta and vegetables to saucepan.

Meanwhile, in a medium saucepan combine tomatoes, jalapeño pepper, margarine, chili powder, and salt. Bring to boiling. Reduce heat to medium and simmer, uncovered, for 8 minutes. Stir in beef; heat through.

Pour tomato mixture over pasta mixture; add cilantro. Toss gently to combine. Transfer to a warm serving dish. Sprinkle with cheese.

Nutrition facts per serving: 409 cal., 13 g total fat (5 g sat. fat), 47 mg chol., 248 mg sodium, 50 g carbo., 5 g fiber, 26 g pro. Daily values: 30% vit. A, 158% vit. C, 14% calcium, 5% iron

red **alert**

Ground red chili and red chili powder are not the same seasoning. Both are hot, but the former is solely ground dried red chili peppers; the latter is usually the same dried red chili peppers along with oregano, cumin, garlic, and salt (the traditional blend for a "bowl of red"), but the mix varies depending on the brand.

- 6 ounces dried wagon wheel macaroni (2¼ cups)
- 12 ounces broccoli, cut up (3 cups)
- 1 cup frozen whole kernel corn
- 3 medium tomatoes, peeled and chopped
- 1 jalapeño pepper, seeded and chopped
- 1 tablespoon margarine or butter
- 2 to 3 teaspoons chili powder
- ⅛ teaspoon salt
- 1 cup chopped cooked beef
- 2 tablespoons snipped fresh cilantro
- ½ cup shredded Monterey Jack cheese with jalapeño peppers, Monterey Jack cheese, or cheddar cheese

linguine with steak & spicy garlic sauce

The lively sauce for this pasta with pepper steak has eight ingredients, and six of them are garlic, so you know it's got to be good (and quick). Buy only plump heads of garlic and store them in a dark, cool, dry spot.

1 9-ounce package refrigerated tomato or red pepper linguine or fettuccine

1 small yellow summer squash or zucchini, halved lengthwise and sliced

1 medium green sweet pepper, cut into bite-size strips (1 cup)

½ teaspoon coarsely ground black pepper

8 ounces beef top loin steak, cut ¾ inch thick

1 tablespoon olive oil or cooking oil

½ cup chicken broth

¼ cup dry white wine

6 cloves garlic, minced

Start to finish: 25 minutes   Makes 4 servings

Cook pasta according to package directions, adding summer squash and sweet pepper the last 2 minutes of cooking; drain. Return pasta and vegetables to saucepan.

Meanwhile, rub black pepper onto both sides of steak. In a large skillet cook steak in hot oil over medium heat to desired doneness, turning once. (Allow 10 to 12 minutes for medium doneness.) Remove meat from the skillet.

For sauce, stir chicken broth, wine, and garlic into skillet. Bring to boiling. Reduce heat and simmer, uncovered, for 2 minutes. Remove skillet from heat.

Cut steak into thin bite-size strips. Pour sauce over pasta mixture; add steak slices. Toss gently to combine. Transfer to a warm serving platter.

Nutrition facts per serving: 247 cal., 13 g total fat (4 g sat. fat), 49 mg chol., 238 mg sodium, 13 g carbo., 1 g fiber, 18 g pro. Daily values: 5% vit. A, 36% vit. C, 6% calcium, 16% iron

tuna & pasta alfredo

When time is precious, remember this tasty dish. One after another, all the sauce ingredients cook in the same pot for maximum flavor and minimal cleanup.

Start to finish: 25 minutes   Makes 6 servings

Cook pasta according to package directions; drain.

Meanwhile, in a large saucepan cook broccoli rabe and sweet pepper in margarine until tender. Stir in Alfredo sauce and dill. If necessary, add milk to make desired consistency. Gently stir in pasta and tuna. Heat through. Transfer to a warm serving dish. If desired, sprinkle with the toasted almonds.

Nutrition facts per serving: 324 cal., 12 g total fat (5 g sat. fat), 39 mg chol., 461 mg sodium, 35 g carbo., 1 g fiber, 19 g pro. Daily values: 49% vit. A, 69% vit. C, 11% calcium, 12% iron

Note: To broil tuna, place on the greased unheated rack of a broiler pan. Broil 4 inches from the heat for 4 to 6 minutes per ½-inch thickness or until fish flakes easily with fork. If fish is more than 1 inch thick, turn it over halfway through cooking. To poach tuna, add 1½ cups water to a large skillet. Bring to boiling; add fish. Simmer, uncovered, for 4 to 6 minutes per ½-inch thickness or until fish flakes easily with fork.

broccoli and then some
Italians relish broccoli rabe (pronounced *rob*), broccoli's pungent, slightly bitter-tasting cousin. Also known as rapini, its small buds look somewhat like those on broccoli, but its stems are slender and its jagged leaves are large in contrast to broccoli's thick stems and small leaves.

3 cups dried mini lasagna, broken mafalda, or medium noodles

2 cups chopped broccoli rabe or broccoli (6 ounces)

1 medium red sweet pepper, chopped

1 tablespoon margarine or butter

1 10-ounce container refrigerated light Alfredo sauce

2 teaspoons snipped fresh dill

1 to 2 tablespoons milk

8 ounces flaked, cooked tuna* or one 9½-ounce can tuna (water pack), drained and broken into chunks

½ cup sliced almonds, toasted (optional)

strawberries, salmon, & fettuccine

Strawberries aren't just for dessert. Partner their delicate sweetness with juicy broiled salmon brushed with raspberry vinaigrette. The reward is a delightful main course for a spring dinner.

Start to finish: 25 minutes   Makes 4 servings

In a small bowl whisk together raspberry vinegar, olive oil, sugar, pepper, and garlic. Reserve 1 tablespoon of the oil mixture; set aside.

Rinse fish; pat dry. Place fish on the greased, unheated rack of a broiler pan; tuck under any thin edges. Brush fish with reserved oil mixture. Broil 4 inches from the heat for 4 to 6 minutes per ½-inch thickness or until fish flakes easily with a fork.

Meanwhile, cook pasta in boiling salted water according to package directions; drain. Return pasta to saucepan. Pour remaining oil mixture over pasta; toss to coat.

Flake cooked salmon. Add salmon and strawberries to pasta; toss gently. Transfer to a warm serving platter. Sprinkle with green onions.

Nutrition facts per serving: 357 cal., 15 g total fat (3 g sat. fat), 70 mg chol., 87 mg sodium, 40 g carbo., 1 g fiber, 17 g pro. Daily values: 8% vit. A, 38% vit. C, 4% calcium, 23% iron

⅓ cup raspberry vinegar

3 tablespoons olive oil

2 teaspoons sugar

¼ teaspoon coarsely ground pepper

1 clove garlic, minced

1 8- to 10-ounce skinless, boneless
    salmon fillet or other fish fillet

1 9-ounce package refrigerated
    spinach or plain fettuccine

1 cup sliced strawberries

¼ cup sliced green onions

pasta with smoked salmon & lemon cream

You can prepare this dish in 20 minutes, hardly longer than it takes to cook the pasta. The elegant result tastes as if preparation had taken hours.

8 ounces dried medium shell macaroni, cavatelli, or orecchiette

1 5-ounce container semisoft cheese with garlic and herbs

⅓ cup milk

1 teaspoon finely shredded lemon peel

1 tablespoon lemon juice

2 medium zucchini and/or yellow summer squash, halved lengthwise and thinly sliced (2 cups)

6 ounces thinly sliced, smoked salmon (lox-style), cut into ½-inch strips

2 tablespoons snipped fresh chives

Start to finish: 20 minutes   Makes 4 servings

Cook pasta according to package directions; drain. Return pasta to saucepan.

Meanwhile, for sauce, in a medium saucepan heat the cheese and milk over low heat until cheese melts, whisking until smooth. Stir in lemon peel and lemon juice. Stir in zucchini and salmon; heat through. Pour sauce over pasta; toss to coat.

Transfer to a warm serving platter. Sprinkle with chives.

Nutrition facts per serving: 420 cal., 15 g total fat (9 g sat. fat), 44 mg chol., 347 mg sodium, 48 g carbo., 1 g fiber, 19 g pro. Daily values: 11% vit. A, 15% vit. C, 6% calcium, 18% iron

the key to lox

Can you tell real lox from a fishy imposter? If it's draped over a cream-cheese-slathered bagel, that's one clue. If you buy it at a Jewish deli, that's another. But most of all, to pass the lox test, those rosy, translucent, paper-thin salmon slices must be brine-cured, with a bold, salty flavor. Nova Scotia smoked salmon (or Nova) is more delicate in flavor (and more expensive).

fusilli with white wine vinaigrette clam sauce

Pasta with clam sauce, a perennial favorite at Italian restaurants, replicates easily at home. This speedy version improves upon the usual renditions with the addition of red sweet pepper and fresh mushrooms.

Start to finish: 20 minutes   Makes 4 servings

Cook pasta according to package directions; drain. Return pasta to saucepan.

Meanwhile, drain clams, reserving juice in a measuring cup. If necessary, add water to juice to make 1 cup. Stir clam juice mixture into cornstarch; stir in wine. Set aside.

For sauce, in a medium skillet cook garlic in hot oil over medium heat for 30 seconds. Add mushrooms and sweet pepper; cook for 1 minute more. Stir in clam juice mixture. Cook and stir until thickened and bubbly. Stir in clams, parsley, and oregano; heat through. Pour sauce over pasta, add cheese, and toss to coat. Serve immediately.

Nutrition facts per serving: 355 cal., 8 g total fat (2 g sat. fat), 62 mg chol., 169 mg sodium, 52 g carbo., 1 g fiber, 19 g pro. Daily values: 16% vit. A, 60% vit. C, 13% calcium, 45% iron

8 ounces dried fusilli

2 6½-ounce cans minced clams

2 teaspoons cornstarch

¼ cup dry white wine or lemon juice

3 cloves garlic, minced

1 tablespoon olive oil or cooking oil

1 cup sliced fresh mushrooms

1 medium red sweet pepper, chopped

3 tablespoons snipped fresh parsley

1 tablespoon snipped fresh oregano

¼ cup grated Parmesan cheese

linguine with fennel & shrimp in orange sauce

Licorice-flavor fennel and the best oranges begin to appear in markets as summer's bounty fades. Serve this easy seafood sauce throughout the cool months to show off its seasonal flavors.

8 ounces dried spinach, tomato-basil, or plain linguine or fettuccine

8 ounces peeled, deveined shrimp

1 medium fennel bulb, trimmed and sliced (about 1½ cups)

1 tablespoon olive oil or cooking oil

1 cup chicken broth

1 tablespoon cornstarch

1 teaspoon finely shredded orange peel

¼ cup orange juice

2 oranges, peeled, cut in half, and sliced crosswise

1 green onion, thinly sliced

Snipped fennel leaves

Start to finish: 25 minutes   Makes 4 servings

Cook pasta according to package directions until nearly tender; add shrimp. Return to boiling. Reduce heat and simmer for 1 to 3 minutes more or until shrimp are opaque and pasta is tender but firm. Drain; return to saucepan.

Meanwhile, for sauce, in a medium saucepan cook fennel in hot oil over medium heat for 3 to 5 minutes or until crisp-tender. In a small bowl stir together chicken broth and cornstarch; add orange peel and orange juice. Add broth mixture to saucepan. Cook and stir until thickened and bubbly. Cook and stir 2 minutes more. Gently stir in orange slices.

Pour sauce over pasta mixture; toss lightly to coat. Transfer to a warm serving dish. Sprinkle with green onion and snipped fennel leaves.

Nutrition facts per serving: 342 cal., 5 g total fat (1 g sat. fat), 87 mg chol., 321 mg sodium, 54 g carbo., 12 g fiber, 20 g pro. Daily values: 14% vit. A, 81% vit. C, 6% calcium, 26% iron

rigatoni with eggplant & dried tomato pesto

Medieval Italians shunned eggplant as they thought it made one mad. Not true, of course, but guests will be wild for this full-flavored pasta sauce—made richer and sweeter with roasted vegetables. (Pictured on the cover.)

1 medium onion, cut into 8 wedges

2 tablespoons olive oil

1 medium eggplant (about 1 pound), halved lengthwise

6 ounces dried rigatoni, penne, or fusilli

⅓ recipe Dried Tomato Pesto

¼ teaspoon coarsely ground pepper

2 tablespoons crumbled goat cheese or feta cheese (optional)

Fresh basil (optional)

Start to finish: 35 minutes   Makes 4 servings

Place onion in a large shallow baking pan; brush with 1 tablespoon of the olive oil. Roast in a 425° oven for 10 minutes; stir. Brush eggplant with remaining olive oil. Place eggplant in pan, cut side down. Roast 15 minutes more or until onion is golden brown and eggplant is tender.

Meanwhile, cook pasta according to package directions; drain. Add Dried Tomato Pesto and pepper to pasta; toss gently to coat. Transfer pasta to a warm serving dish; keep warm.

Cut eggplant into ½-inch-thick slices. Toss eggplant and onion with pasta; season to taste with salt. If desired, top with cheese and basil.

Dried Tomato Pesto: Drain ¾ cup oil-packed dried tomatoes, reserving oil. Add enough olive oil to make ½ cup; set aside. Place tomatoes, ¼ cup pine nuts or slivered almonds, ¼ cup snipped fresh basil, ½ teaspoon salt, and 8 cloves garlic, chopped, in a food processor bowl. Cover; process until finely chopped. With machine running, gradually add the oil, processing until almost smooth. Divide pesto into thirds. Refrigerate or freeze unused portions. Makes approximately three ⅓-cup portions.

Nutrition facts per serving: 370 cal., 19 g total fat (3 g sat. fat), 0 mg chol., 112 mg sodium, 43 g carbo., 4 g fiber, 8 g pro. Daily values: 1% vit. A, 16% vit. C, 2% calcium, 16% iron

pasta with chèvre

Recover from rush hour over a bright, easy-going Mediterranean mélange. Here, pasta shells pair with tangy goat cheese, meaty olives, juicy tomatoes, yellow sweet peppers, and aromatic basil. (Pictured on front cover flap.)

Start to finish: 25 minutes   Makes 4 servings

Cook pasta according to package directions; drain. Return pasta to saucepan.

Add tomatoes, sweet pepper, cheese, olives, basil, and olive oil to saucepan. Toss gently to combine. Transfer to a warm serving dish. If desired, sprinkle with black pepper.

Nutrition facts per serving: 402 cal., 18 g total fat (5 g sat. fat), 25 mg chol., 216 mg sodium, 49 g carbo., 1 g fiber, 14 g pro. Daily values: 8% vit. A, 96% vit. C, 4% calcium, 18% iron

oh, those **olives**

If your olives come only from a can or speared from the depths of a martini, you're missing a world of good eating. Olives grow on six continents and are cured and dressed in countless ways. Specialty food stores and even some supermarkets now offer them in an exciting variety—fat, slender, round, tapered, black, brown, green, purple, smooth, wrinkled, salt-cured, brine-cured, oil-cured—in bulk and prepackaged. Ask for suggestions and for samples, if possible. It's the best way to choose.

8   ounces dried cavatelli, conchiglie, or gnocco

2   medium tomatoes, chopped

1   yellow sweet pepper, cut into bite-size pieces

4   ounces crumbled semisoft mild goat cheese (chèvre) or crumbled feta cheese

⅓   cup pitted, chopped Greek black (kalamata) olives or ripe olives

2   tablespoons snipped fresh basil

2   tablespoons olive oil

¼   teaspoon coarsely ground black pepper (optional)

penne with broccoli & dried tomatoes

Is this Italian? Or is it Chinese? With flavors borrowed from both cuisines, this hearty vegetable main course should please about everyone.

Start to finish: 25 minutes   Makes 4 servings

Cook pasta according to package directions, adding broccoli the last 2 minutes of cooking; drain. Return pasta and broccoli to saucepan.

Meanwhile, drain tomatoes, reserving 2 tablespoons oil. Cut tomatoes into strips.

In a saucepan cook mushrooms, crushed red pepper, and garlic in reserved oil for 3 to 4 minutes or until mushrooms are tender. Stir in basil. Add to pasta along with tomato strips; toss gently to combine. Transfer to a warm serving dish. If desired, sprinkle with cheese.

Nutrition facts per serving: 348 cal., 10 g total fat (1 g sat. fat), 0 mg chol., 70 mg sodium, 55 g carbo., 5 g fiber, 12 g pro. Daily values: 18% vit. A, 166% vit. C, 6% calcium, 23% iron

- **8 ounces dried tomato-basil penne or plain ziti (2¼ cups)**
- **4 cups broccoli flowerets**
- **½ cup oil-packed dried tomatoes**
- **1 cup sliced fresh shiitake mushrooms**
- **¼ teaspoon crushed red pepper**
- **3 cloves garlic, minced**
- **½ cup snipped fresh basil**
- **Shredded Parmesan cheese (optional)**

tomatoes & ravioli
with escarole

Serve meat-filled tortellini cloaked in a chunky tomato sauce and suit hectic schedules and hearty appetites to a T. Adding leafy escarole, a winter staple, satisfies palates that crave something fresh and green.

Start to finish: 30 minutes   Makes 4 servings

For sauce, in a large skillet cook onion and garlic in hot oil 2 minutes. Add mushrooms, tomatoes, and chicken broth. Bring to boiling. Reduce heat and simmer, uncovered, about 7 minutes or until mushrooms are tender and sauce is slightly reduced (you should have about 3 cups sauce). Add escarole, basil, and rosemary, stirring just until the escarole is wilted.

Meanwhile, cook pasta according to package directions; drain. Return pasta to saucepan. Pour sauce over pasta; toss to coat. Transfer to a warm serving dish. Sprinkle with pine nuts.

Nutrition facts per serving: 339 cal., 14 g total fat (3 g sat. fat), 34 mg chol., 454 mg sodium, 43 g carbo., 4 g fiber, 16 g pro. Daily values: 19% vit. A, 46% vit. C, 7% calcium, 29% iron

½	cup chopped onion
2	cloves garlic, minced
1	tablespoon olive oil or cooking oil
3	cups sliced fresh mushrooms
2	cups chopped plum tomatoes
¾	cup chicken broth
4	cups coarsely chopped escarole
1	tablespoon snipped fresh basil
1	teaspoon snipped fresh rosemary
1	9-ounce package refrigerated meat-filled ravioli
¼	cup pine nuts, toasted

escarole essentials
With its sturdy green leaves and pungent flavor, escarole adds texture, color, and punch to hearty one-pot meals or wilted salads. This relative of endive is slightly chewy and very tasty. Spinach is an acceptable substitute when escarole is scarce (although it's milder in flavor and less crisp).

angel hair with asparagus, tomatoes, & basil

The Italians are poetic when it comes to naming pastas, and maestros at creating sauces for them. A fine example is this simple yet eloquent composition of crunchy asparagus, vine-ripened tomatoes, and fresh basil.

16 fresh asparagus spears

1 9-ounce package refrigerated angel hair pasta

4 cloves garlic, minced

¼ teaspoon pepper

1 tablespoon olive oil

6 medium plum tomatoes, seeded and chopped (2¼ cups)

¼ cup dry white wine

¼ teaspoon salt

1 tablespoon butter*

¼ cup snipped fresh basil

Start to finish: 20 minutes   Makes 3 servings

Trim asparagus; rinse in cold water. Remove tips; set tips aside. Bias-slice remaining asparagus stalks into 1- to 1½-inch pieces; set stalks aside.

Cook pasta according to package directions; drain. Return pasta to saucepan.

Meanwhile, in a large skillet cook and stir garlic and pepper in hot oil for 1 minute. Add tomatoes; cook for 2 minutes more, stirring often.

Add asparagus stalks, wine, and salt to skillet. Cook, uncovered, for 3 minutes. Add asparagus tips. Cook, uncovered, for 1 minute more. Add butter, stirring until melted. Add asparagus mixture and basil to pasta; toss gently to coat. Transfer to a warm serving dish.

Nutrition facts per serving: 484 cal., 11 g total fat (3 g sat. fat), 10 mg chol., 238 mg sodium, 81 g carbo., 4 g fiber, 15 g pro. Daily values: 19% vit. A, 86% vit. C, 5% calcium, 31% iron

Note: The butter in this recipe binds the sauce. Margarine might not be an effective substitute in making this dish.

tortellini, green & simple

In an ages-old Italian name game, these stuffed half-moons are called "tortellini" in Bologna, "tortelli" in Florence, and "cappelletti" elsewhere. You'll call them fresh, fast, and delicious!

Start to finish: 20 minutes   Makes 3 servings

Cook pasta according to package directions, adding peas and broccoli to the water with pasta; drain. Return pasta and vegetables to saucepan.

Add shredded cheese, olive oil, oregano, and crushed red pepper to pasta mixture; toss to coat. Transfer to a warm serving dish.

Nutrition facts per serving: 368 cal., 14 g total fat (4 g sat. fat), 51 mg chol., 419 mg sodium, 45 g carbo., 3 g fiber, 18 g pro. Daily values: 15% vit. A, 68% vit. C, 19% calcium, 18% iron

- 1 9-ounce package refrigerated meat- or cheese-filled tortellini
- ½ cup frozen peas
- 1 cup broccoli flowerets
- ¼ cup shredded fontina or Swiss cheese (1 ounce)
- 1 tablespoon olive oil
- 2 teaspoons snipped fresh oregano
- ¼ teaspoon crushed red pepper

roasted red pepper sauce over tortellini

For leisurely dining, start in the fast lane. Take advantage of ready-to-use roasted peppers and tortellini to speed up meal preparation. Then, slow down and enjoy the delectable result. The sauce is equally tasty spooned over chicken or fish.

1 **9-ounce package refrigerated meat- or cheese-filled tortellini**

1 **12-ounce jar roasted red sweet peppers, drained**

½ **cup chopped onion**

3 **cloves garlic, minced**

1 **tablespoon margarine or butter**

2 **teaspoons snipped fresh thyme or ½ teaspoon dried thyme, crushed**

2 **teaspoons snipped fresh oregano or ¼ teaspoon dried oregano, crushed**

1 **teaspoon sugar**

Start to finish: 20 minutes   Makes 3 servings

Cook pasta according to package directions; drain. Return to saucepan.

Meanwhile, place roasted sweet peppers in a food processor bowl. Cover and process until smooth. Set aside.

For sauce, in a medium saucepan cook the onion and garlic in hot margarine until tender. Add pureed peppers, thyme, oregano, and sugar. Cook and stir until heated through. Pour sauce over pasta; toss to coat. Transfer to a warm serving dish.

Nutrition facts per serving: 343 cal., 15 g total fat (4 g sat. fat), 75 mg chol., 298 mg sodium, 40 g carbo., 2 g fiber, 14 g pro. Daily values: 43% vit. A, 343% vit. C, 4% calcium, 25% iron

linguine with gorgonzola sauce

Look no further for a quick and certain antidote to car pools and commutes than this luscious, creamy-crunchy concoction of pungent Gorgonzola, fresh asparagus, and toasted nuts.

1 9-ounce package refrigerated linguine

1 pound asparagus, cut into 1-inch pieces

1 cup half-and-half or light cream

½ cup crumbled Gorgonzola or other blue cheese (2 ounces)

2 tablespoons chopped walnuts, toasted

Crumbled Gorgonzola or other blue cheese (optional)

Start to finish: 20 minutes   Makes 3 servings

Cook pasta according to package directions, adding asparagus to the water with pasta; drain. Return pasta and asparagus to pan.

Meanwhile, in a medium saucepan combine half-and-half and Gorgonzola cheese. Bring to boiling over medium heat. Reduce heat and simmer for 3 minutes.

Pour sauce over pasta mixture; toss gently to coat. Transfer to a warm serving dish. Sprinkle with nuts. If desired, top with additional Gorgonzola cheese.

Nutrition facts per serving: 478 cal., 22 g total fat (10 g sat. fat), 62 mg chol., 365 mg sodium, 54 g carbo., 2 g fiber, 19 g pro. Daily values: 22% vit. A, 40% vit. C, 19% calcium, 12% iron

the skinny on cream sauce

This recipe creates a delectable cream sauce with a rich flavor and velvety texture—but less fat—by substituting half-and-half or light cream for the usual heavy cream. Both products thicken beautifully when briefly simmered in an open pan, a classic technique for sauces known as reducing.

chunky garden pasta sauce

Rediscover ever-popular pasta primavera, done over in the richer flavors and deeper colors of autumn and just as fresh and easy. Sop up the delicious sauce with a crusty country bread.

Start to finish: 30 minutes   Makes 4 servings

For sauce, in a large saucepan stir together the undrained tomatoes, mushrooms, tomato sauce, chopped fennel, carrots, sweet pepper, wine, and fennel leaves.

Bring to boiling. Reduce heat and simmer, covered, for 10 minutes. Uncover and simmer 5 to 10 minutes more or until desired consistency.

Meanwhile, cook pasta according to package directions; drain. Return to saucepan. Pour sauce over pasta, tossing to coat. Serve immediately.

Nutrition facts per serving: 324 cal., 2 g total fat (0 g sat. fat), 0 mg chol., 571 mg sodium, 64 g carbo., 8 g fiber, 12 g pro. Daily values: 60% vit. A, 85% vit. C, 92% calcium, 27% iron

Note: For a meat sauce, cook 12 ounces ground beef or bulk pork sausage and drain well. Stir into the sauce just before spooning over the pasta.

- 1 14½-ounce can diced tomatoes with garlic, oregano, and basil, undrained
- 1 14½-ounce can low-sodium tomatoes, undrained and cut up
- 1½ cups sliced fresh mushrooms
- 1 8-ounce can low-sodium tomato sauce
- ¾ cup chopped fennel
- ½ cup coarsely shredded carrots
- ½ cup chopped green sweet pepper
- ¼ cup dry red wine
- 1 tablespoon snipped fresh fennel leaves
- 8 ounces dried spaghetti

fresh tomato fusilli

What to serve on balmy evenings, when life slows and moves outdoors? Light and easy pasta is an obvious choice, with the season's ambrosial tomatoes, which need very little else to show them off.

Start to finish: 25 minutes   Makes 4 servings

Cook pasta according to package directions; drain. Return pasta to pan.

Meanwhile, for sauce, in a large skillet cook mushrooms, onion, and garlic in hot oil about 5 minutes or until tender. Stir chicken broth into flour; add to mushroom mixture. Cook and stir over medium heat until slightly thickened and bubbly. Cook and stir 1 minute more. Stir in tomatoes, prosciutto, basil, and oregano. Pour over pasta; toss to coat.

Transfer to a warm serving dish. Sprinkle with Parmesan cheese.

Nutrition facts per serving: 363 cal., 9 g total fat (1 g sat. fat), 5 mg chol., 364 mg sodium, 56 g carbo., 3 g fiber, 16 g pro. Daily values: 7% vit. A, 41% vit. C, 7% calcium, 28% iron

8 ounces dried fusilli

4 cups sliced fresh mushrooms

¼ cup chopped onion

1 clove garlic, minced

1 tablespoon olive oil or cooking oil

¾ cup chicken broth

1 teaspoon all-purpose flour

2 cups red and/or yellow cherry tomatoes, halved

¼ cup finely chopped prosciutto or cooked ham

2 tablespoons snipped fresh basil

1 tablespoon snipped fresh oregano

¼ cup shredded Parmesan cheese

garganelli with asparagus cheese sauce

The first slender asparagus announces spring's arrival as reliably as a calendar. Why not share the good news with this easy, vibrant sauce and the ribbed pasta tubes known as garganelli.

- 8 ounces dried garganelli or large bow ties

- 1 pound fresh asparagus, cut into 2-inch pieces

- 1 8-ounce package reduced-fat cream cheese (Neufchâtel), cut up

- ¾ cup milk

- ⅛ teaspoon white or black pepper

- ¼ cup shredded Parmesan cheese

- 2 teaspoons snipped fresh thyme, tarragon, basil, or chives

- 2 tablespoons sliced almonds or chopped walnuts, toasted (optional)

- Snipped fresh thyme, tarragon, basil, or chives (optional)

Start to finish: 25 minutes   Makes 4 servings

Cook pasta according to package directions, adding asparagus the last 5 minutes of cooking; drain. Return pasta and asparagus to saucepan.

Meanwhile, for sauce, in a medium saucepan heat the cream cheese, milk, and pepper over medium-low heat, whisking occasionally until cream cheese melts. Stir in Parmesan cheese and the 2 teaspoons desired herb; heat through. (If sauce seems too thick, stir in additional milk to make desired consistency.)

Pour sauce over pasta mixture; toss to coat. Transfer to a warm serving dish. If desired, sprinkle with nuts and garnish with additional herb.

Nutrition facts per serving: 403 cal., 18 g total fat (9 g sat. fat), 99 mg chol., 329 mg sodium, 43 g carbo., 2 g fiber, 18 g pro. Daily values: 28% vit. A, 35% vit. C, 13% calcium, 20% iron

mostaccioli & sicilian tomato sauce

No need to work hard in the kitchen when the temperature rises. In fact, with this garden pesto sauce, you hardly have to cook: Just whirl the fresh ingredients in a food processor and spoon over slender pasta tubes.

Start to finish: 25 minutes   Makes 4 servings

Cook pasta according to package directions; drain. Return pasta to pan.

Meanwhile, for sauce, in a food processor bowl combine pine nuts, cheese, and garlic. Cover and process until chopped. Add about half of the basil and all of the oil. Cover and process until basil is chopped, stopping the machine occasionally to scrape the sides. Add remaining basil and repeat. Add tomatoes. Cover and process with several on/off turns until the tomatoes are just chunky. (If mixture is too smooth, add some additional chopped tomato.) Stir in salt and pepper.

Pour sauce over pasta; toss to coat. Or, if you prefer a warm sauce, pour sauce into a saucepan; heat through.

Nutrition facts per serving: 459 cal., 22 g total fat (4 g sat. fat), 5 mg chol., 400 mg sodium, 55 g carbo., 3 g fiber, 14 g pro. Daily values: 11% vit. A, 55% vit. C, 12% calcium, 26% iron

- 8 **ounces dried mostaccioli or penne**
- ¼ **cup pine nuts or chopped almonds**
- ¼ **cup grated firm pecorino or Parmesan cheese**
- 2 **cloves garlic, minced**
- 2 **cups loosely packed fresh basil leaves, chopped**
- ¼ **cup olive oil**
- 1½ **pounds ripe tomatoes, peeled, seeded, and cut into chunks**
- ½ **teaspoon salt**
- ⅛ **teaspoon pepper**

snappy
pasta
salads

turkey & pasta salad

It's Waldorf salad with a twist! This delicious version builds on the classic, but goes modern with smoked turkey, raspberries, and curly rotini pasta—and lightens up with a low-fat dressing.

Start to finish: 25 minutes   Makes 4 servings

Cook pasta according to package directions; drain. Rinse with cold water; drain again.

Toss chopped apple with lime juice or lemon juice. In a large mixing bowl combine pasta, chopped apple, turkey, raspberries, and celery.

For dressing, in a small mixing bowl combine yogurt, mayonnaise dressing, milk, mustard, marjoram, and celery seed. Drizzle dressing over pasta mixture; toss gently to coat.

Nutrition facts per serving: 278 cal., 2 g total fat (0 g sat. fat), 25 mg chol., 820 mg sodium, 45 g carbo., 3 g fiber, 19 g pro. Daily values: 1% vit. A, 19% vit. C, 5% calcium, 17% iron

- 6 ounces dried rotini or radiatore
- 1 medium apple, chopped
- 1 tablespoon lime or lemon juice
- ½ pound smoked turkey breast, cut into bite-size pieces
- 1 cup raspberries or strawberries, cut in quarters
- ½ cup sliced celery
- ¼ cup plain fat-free yogurt
- 2 tablespoons fat-free mayonnaise dressing or salad dressing
- 2 tablespoons skim milk
- 4 teaspoons Dijon-style mustard
- 1 tablespoon snipped fresh marjoram
- ¼ teaspoon celery seed

sweet & tangy turkey salad

The perfect sauce for turkey is not always the holiday gravy. Here, an unexpected tart-sweet salad dressing, made with just two ingredients plus a sprinkle of salt and pepper, gives new life to a traditional favorite.

1½ cups dried tricolor or plain rotini

½ cup plain low-fat yogurt or light mayonnaise dressing or salad dressing

2 tablespoons apricot preserves or jam

⅛ teaspoon salt

⅛ teaspoon pepper

8 ounces smoked cooked turkey or chicken breast, cut into bite-size cubes (1½ cups)

1 cup coarsely shredded carrots

1 cup cubed, peeled jicama or thinly sliced celery

1 cup cherry tomatoes, quartered

¼ cup thinly sliced green onions

Lettuce leaves

Start to finish: 25 minutes   Makes 4 servings

Cook pasta according to package directions; drain. Rinse with cold water; drain again.

In a large mixing bowl stir together yogurt, preserves, salt, and pepper. Add pasta, turkey, carrots, jicama, tomatoes, and green onions. Toss gently to coat.

To serve, arrange lettuce leaves on plates. Top with salad.

Nutrition facts per serving: 239 cal., 3 g total fat (1 g sat. fat), 31 mg chol., 677 mg sodium, 37 g carbo., 2 g fiber, 17 g pro. Daily values: 82% vit. A, 37% vit. C, 6% calcium, 13% iron

chicken-pasta salad with cilantro dressing

While its name gives no clue, this lively, low-fuss salad hails from the blazing Southwest, where fiery peppers rule. The bold, cilantro-flecked dressing radiates the region's signature flavor. Turn the heat up or down with more or less jalapeño pepper.

Start to finish: 25 minutes   Makes 4 servings

Cook pasta according to package directions, adding corn the last 2 minutes of cooking; drain. Rinse with cold water; drain again.

Combine the pasta mixture, chicken, carrots, and olives. Pour Cilantro Dressing over pasta mixture. Toss lightly to coat. Serve immediately or cover and chill up to 24 hours.

To serve, divide salad greens among individual plates. Top with pasta mixture.

Cilantro Dressing: In a screw-top jar combine ¼ cup lime juice; ¼ cup snipped fresh cilantro; ¼ cup finely chopped red onion; 3 tablespoons olive oil or salad oil; 1 fresh or canned jalapeño pepper, seeded and finely chopped; and 1 clove garlic, minced. Cover and shake well. Makes about ⅔ cup.

Nutrition facts per serving: 358 cal., 21 g total fat (4 g sat. fat), 41 mg chol., 450 mg sodium, 31 g carbo., 2 g fiber, 15 g pro. Daily values: 10% vit. A, 47% vit. C, 3% calcium, 14% iron

- 1 **cup dried tricolor rotini or gemelli**
- 1 **cup frozen whole kernel corn**
- 8 **ounces smoked cooked chicken or turkey breast, cut in bite-size strips (1½ cups)**
- 1 **cup thinly sliced carrots or bite-size jicama strips**
- ½ **cup pitted ripe olives, halved**
- 1 **recipe Cilantro Dressing**
- 4 **cups torn mixed salad greens**

teriyaki chicken noodle salad

This fresh chicken salad is "fast food" in the best possible sense. The crunchy noodles and mixture of Asian spices that enliven the dressing come ready-to-use in a package of ramen-style soup.

1	3-ounce package chicken- or Oriental-flavor ramen noodles
¼	cup rice vinegar or white wine vinegar
2	tablespoons orange juice
2	tablespoons salad oil
	Few dashes bottled hot pepper sauce
6	cups torn mixed salad greens
2	cups fresh vegetables such as bean sprouts, halved pea pods, or sliced carrots, yellow summer squash, zucchini, cucumber, and/or onions
2	oranges, peeled, halved, and thinly sliced
12	ounces skinless, boneless chicken breast halves
2	tablespoons cooking oil
	Coarsely ground black pepper

Start to finish: 30 minutes   Makes 4 servings

For dressing, in a screw-top jar combine the flavor packet from the ramen noodles, vinegar, orange juice, salad oil, and hot pepper sauce. Cover and shake well; set aside.

In a large salad bowl combine salad greens, desired vegetables, and orange slices; toss gently to mix. Break ramen noodles into pieces; add to salad. Cover and chill up to 1 hour.

Meanwhile, rinse chicken; pat dry. Cut chicken into thin bite-size strips. Pour cooking oil in a wok or large skillet. Preheat over medium-high heat. Add chicken; stir-fry for 2 to 3 minutes or until no longer pink.

While chicken is cooking, pour the dressing over the salad mixture; toss gently to coat. Let stand about 5 minutes to soften noodles, tossing occasionally.

Add chicken and pan juices to salad; toss gently. Sprinkle with pepper. Serve immediately.

Nutrition facts per serving: 351 cal., 17 g total fat (3 g sat. fat), 45 mg chol., 521 mg sodium, 30 g carbo., 4 g fiber, 21 g pro. Daily values: 5% vit. A, 94% vit. C, 5% calcium, 16% iron

curried ham & pasta salad

Get a quick fix on curry with this substantial salad. It evokes traditional Indian flavors, but puts preparation on fast forward by blending hot-sweet mango chutney, spicy curry powder, and cooling yogurt right into the dressing.

2 cups dried cavatelli or small shell macaroni (6 ounces)

2 cups broccoli flowerets

1½ cups cubed cooked ham

½ cup coarsely shredded carrot

½ cup plain yogurt, mayonnaise, or salad dressing

½ cup chutney or apricot spreadable fruit

1 teaspoon curry powder

Lettuce or spinach leaves

½ cup slivered almonds, toasted (optional)

Start to finish: 25 minutes   Makes 4 servings

Cook pasta according to package directions; drain. Rinse with cold water; drain again.

In a large bowl stir together pasta, broccoli, ham, and carrot; set aside.

For dressing, in a small bowl stir together yogurt, chutney, and curry powder. Pour dressing over pasta mixture; toss gently to coat. Serve immediately or cover and chill up to 24 hours.

To serve, arrange lettuce leaves on plates. Top with salad. If desired, sprinkle with almonds.

Nutrition facts per serving: 394 cal., 4 g total fat (1 g sat. fat), 31 mg chol., 745 mg sodium, 65 g carbo., 3 g fiber, 23 g pro. Daily values: 48% vit. A, 44% vit. C, 7% calcium, 22% iron

choose a **chutney,** then relish the **possibilities**

A condiment for Indian curries, sweet-tart chutney (Hindi for "strongly spiced") also sparks simple poultry dishes, salads, and sandwiches. Pick a favorite among these rich jams concocted of chopped fruit (mango is classic), vegetables, and spices enlivened with hot peppers, fresh ginger, or vinegar, and keep a jar on hand for a quick mealtime fix.

gingered beef & pasta salad

Become a quick-change artist! When toasted sesame oil, rice vinegar, soy sauce, and fresh ginger replace the usual mayonnaise dressing, a simple beef salad reinvents itself as something altogether new and exotic.

Start to finish: 30 minutes   Makes 4 servings

Cook pasta according to package directions; drain. Rinse with cold water; drain again.

In a large salad bowl combine the pasta, mesclun, beef, and tomatoes.

Meanwhile, in a small saucepan stir together soy sauce, vinegar, water, gingerroot, sugar, and sesame oil. Bring to a boil, stirring to dissolve sugar. Remove from heat and pour over the salad. Toss gently to coat. Serve immediately.

Nutrition facts per serving: 276 cal., 5 g total fat (2 g sat. fat), 30 mg chol., 550 mg sodium, 39 g carbo., 2 g fiber, 18 g pro. Daily values: 5% vit. A, 21% vit. C, 2% calcium, 22% iron

6 ounces dried radiatore or large bow ties (2 cups)

4 cups mesclun or torn mixed salad greens

6 ounces cooked beef, cubed or cut into bite-size strips (1 cup)

1 cup cherry tomatoes, halved, or one large tomato, cut into wedges

2 tablespoons soy sauce

1 tablespoon rice vinegar or white wine vinegar

1 tablespoon water

2 teaspoons grated gingerroot

1 teaspoon sugar

½ teaspoon toasted sesame oil

orzo salad with herb vinaigrette

It's truly dinner on the double when all you need to do is toss cooked beef, fresh vegetables, and tiny orzo in a prepared herb vinaigrette. Follow with purchased lemon sorbet and almond biscotti for an almost effortless menu.

1 cup orzo

1 teaspoon instant chicken bouillon granules

1 clove garlic, minced

2 cups cubed cooked beef

2 cups chopped plum tomatoes

1¼ cups chopped, seeded cucumber

¼ cup thinly sliced red onion

⅓ cup bottled herb vinaigrette salad dressing or bottled oil and vinegar salad dressing

Butterhead lettuce leaves or spinach leaves

Start to finish: 25 minutes   Makes 4 servings

In a medium saucepan cook pasta according to package directions, adding bouillon granules and garlic to the cooking water; drain. Rinse with cold water; drain again.

In a large bowl toss together pasta mixture, beef, tomatoes, cucumber, and onion. Add salad dressing; toss gently to coat.

To serve, arrange lettuce leaves on plates. Top with salad.

Nutrition facts per serving: 449 cal., 19 g total fat (4 g sat. fat), 61 mg chol., 556 mg sodium, 42 g carbo., 2 g fiber, 28 g pro. Daily values: 7% vit. A, 40% vit. C, 2% calcium, 29% iron

peppered beef
with mostaccioli

When it's supper and the VCR, not dinner and a movie, this supremely easy meat-and-pasta salad gets high ratings for one-stop-shopping convenience.

Start to finish: 25 minutes   Makes 4 servings

Cook pasta according to package directions; drain. Rinse with cold water; drain again.

In a large bowl combine pasta, sweet pepper, salad dressing, and pepper. Toss gently to coat; set aside.

To serve, divide spinach among individual plates. Arrange beef atop spinach. Top with pasta mixture; sprinkle with tomatoes.

Nutrition facts per serving: 337 cal., 6 g total fat (2 g sat. fat), 35 mg chol., 442 mg sodium, 53 g carbo., 3 g fiber, 19 g pro. Daily values: 62% vit. A, 69% vit. C, 10% calcium, 38% iron

53

2 cups dried mostaccioli or rigatoni (8 ounces)

1 medium yellow sweet pepper, coarsely chopped (¾ cup)

½ cup bottled reduced-calorie blue cheese salad dressing

½ teaspoon coarsely ground black pepper

6 cups torn fresh spinach

4 ounces deli peppered beef, cut into bite-size strips

1 cup cherry tomatoes, halved

warm scallop salad with toasted sesame dressing

Sesame seeds turn nutty, crunchy, and golden in minutes in a skillet. If you have access to an Asian market, you can buy them already toasted to save a step.

Start to finish: 30 minutes Makes 4 servings

Cook pasta according to package directions; drain. Rinse with cold water; drain again. In a large mixing bowl toss together pasta, cabbage, and onions. Divide mixture among individual plates.

Meanwhile, for dressing, in a small mixing bowl stir together vinegar, 2 tablespoons of the oil, the soy sauce, honey, and crushed red pepper. Set aside.

In a skillet cook and stir sesame seed over medium heat about 5 minutes or until toasted; set aside.

Add remaining 1 tablespoon oil to skillet; add scallops or shrimp. Cook and stir about 2 minutes or until opaque. If desired, place romaine leaves atop pasta mixture on plates. Place the scallops or shrimp in romaine leaves. Drizzle dressing over all and sprinkle with toasted sesame seed.

Nutrition facts per serving: 425 cal., 14 g total fat (2 g sat. fat), 25 mg chol., 656 mg sodium, 54 g carbo., 2 g fiber, 21 g pro. Daily values: 21% vit. A, 46% vit. C, 11% calcium, 33% iron

2½ cups dried gemelli (8 ounces)

6 cups shredded Chinese cabbage and/or shredded romaine

4 green onions, thinly sliced

¼ cup rice vinegar or white wine vinegar

3 tablespoons salad oil

2 tablespoons soy sauce

1 tablespoon honey

½ teaspoon crushed red pepper

2 tablespoons black or white sesame seed

12 ounces sea scallops or peeled, deveined medium shrimp

4 romaine leaves (optional)

shrimp salad
with dill dressing

Use fresh dill, when you can find it, for its refreshing fragrance and bright flavor. Trim the feathery leaves with scissors, holding a stalk over a bowl and snipping off what you need.

56

1½ cups dried rotini or medium shell macaroni

8 ounces peeled and deveined shrimp

1 tablespoon snipped fresh dill or ½ teaspoon dried dillweed

⅓ cup bottled nonfat white wine vinaigrette salad dressing

2 ounces smoked Gouda cheese, cut into ½-inch cubes, or ½ cup crumbled feta cheese

1 cup shredded fresh spinach

1 cup cherry tomatoes, halved

Fresh spinach leaves (optional)

Start to finish: 25 minutes   Makes 4 servings

Cook pasta according to package directions, adding shrimp the last 3 minutes of cooking; drain. Rinse with cold water; drain again.

Meanwhile, for dressing, stir dill into bottled salad dressing; set aside.

In a large bowl toss together the pasta mixture and cheese. Pour dressing over salad mixture; toss gently to combine. Serve immediately or cover and refrigerate for up to 24 hours.

To serve, stir in shredded spinach and cherry tomatoes. If desired, serve on spinach-lined plates.

Nutrition facts per serving: 240 cal., 5 g total fat (3 g sat. fat), 104 mg chol., 488 mg sodium, 29 g carbo., 1 g fiber, 18 g pro. Daily values: 18% vit. A, 25% vit. C, 11% calcium, 21% iron

tuna-pasta salad with pesto vinaigrette

No tired canned tuna or mayonnaise from a jar here. Instead, combine fresh tuna fillets and a vinaigrette with Provençal flair—definitely a must-try for tuna salad fans.

Start to finish: 20 minutes   Makes 4 servings

In a medium skillet bring water, lemon juice, and peppercorns to boiling; add tuna. Cover; simmer for 8 to 10 minutes or until fish flakes easily with a fork. Drain fish; break into small chunks. Cover; chill.

Cook pasta according to package directions, adding asparagus the last 2 minutes of cooking; drain. Rinse with cold water; drain again. Combine pasta mixture, cucumber, and radishes. Carefully stir in tuna. Drizzle with Pesto Vinaigrette; toss gently to coat.

To serve, divide salad greens among individual plates. Top with salad.

Pesto Vinaigrette: In a small bowl whisk together ½ cup bottled nonfat white wine vinaigrette salad dressing and 2 tablespoons pesto.

Nutrition facts per serving: 435 cal., 23 g total fat (3 g sat. fat), 22 mg chol., 670 mg sodium, 35 g carbo., 2 g fiber, 21 g pro. Daily values: 42% vit. A, 31% vit. C, 3% calcium, 17% iron

- 1 **cup water**
- 2 **tablespoons lemon juice**
- ½ **teaspoon whole black peppercorns**
- 8 **ounces tuna fillets**
- 1½ **cups dried medium shell macaroni (4 ounces)**
- 8 **ounces fresh asparagus, cut into 1-inch pieces (about 1 cup)**
- 1 **cup chopped, seeded cucumber**
- ½ **cup sliced radishes**
- 1 **recipe Pesto Vinaigrette**
- 4 **cups torn mixed salad greens**

penne salad with italian beans & gorgonzola

Assertive blue-veined Gorgonzola, tart sorrel, and bitter radicchio lose some attitude, but not their tasty sass, paired with meaty green beans, pasta, and a mellow herb dressing.

59

Start to finish: 25 minutes   Makes 4 servings

Cook pasta according to package directions, adding green beans the last 5 to 7 minutes of cooking; drain. Rinse pasta and beans with cold water; drain again.

In a large bowl combine Italian salad dressing, tarragon, and pepper. Add pasta mixture and radicchio; toss gently to coat.

To serve, divide sorrel leaves among individual plates. Top with salad. Sprinkle each serving with Gorgonzola cheese.

Nutrition facts per serving: 269 cal., 6 g total fat (3 g sat. fat), 13 mg chol., 566 mg sodium, 42 g carbo., 3 g fiber, 12 g pro. Daily values: 45% vit. A, 38% vit. C, 15% calcium, 26% iron

Note: One 9-ounce package frozen Italian green beans, thawed, may be substituted for the fresh beans. Add frozen and thawed beans to the boiling pasta the last 3 to 4 minutes of cooking.

6 ounces dried penne, ziti, or elbow macaroni

8 ounces Italian green beans, trimmed and bias-sliced into 1-inch pieces*

⅓ cup bottled nonfat Italian salad dressing

1 tablespoon snipped fresh tarragon or ½ teaspoon dried tarragon, crushed

½ teaspoon freshly ground pepper

2 cups torn radicchio or 1 cup finely shredded red cabbage

4 cups fresh sorrel or spinach leaves

½ cup crumbled Gorgonzola or other blue cheese (2 ounces)

fontina & melon salad

Put the "lazy" back in Sundays. Organize brunch around a new take on the fruit-and-cheese course, made in a flash with bottled poppy seed dressing. Accompany with mimosas, the Sunday paper, and a cushiony chair.

1½ cups dried large bow ties
(about 6 ounces)

2 cups cantaloupe and/or
honeydew melon chunks

1 cup cubed fontina or Swiss
cheese (4 ounces)

⅓ cup bottled nonfat poppy seed
salad dressing

1 to 2 tablespoons snipped
fresh mint

2 cups watercress, stems
removed

Start to finish: 25 minutes   Makes 4 servings

Cook pasta according to package directions; drain. Rinse with cold water; drain again.

In a large bowl toss together pasta, cantaloupe, and cheese. Combine salad dressing and mint; pour over pasta mixture, tossing gently to coat. Serve immediately or cover and chill up to 24 hours.

To serve, stir watercress into pasta mixture. If desired, serve salad in melon shells.

Nutrition facts per serving: 319 cal., 11 g total fat (6 g sat. fat), 73 mg chol., 309 mg sodium, 41 g carbo., 1 g fiber, 14 g pro. Daily values: 44% vit. A, 105% vit. C, 18% calcium, 15% iron

tortellini caesar salad

Hail Caesar! Credit bottled Caesar dressing and prepared cheese tortellini for the simplest, most delicious version yet of everybody's favorite salad. Rub an extra clove of garlic inside the salad bowl to transfer its lively flavor to all the fixings.

1 9-ounce package refrigerated cheese-filled tortellini

⅓ cup bottled Caesar salad dressing

1 tablespoon lemon juice

1 clove garlic, minced

6 cups torn romaine

2 tart medium apples, cored and cut into thin wedges, or 2 medium tomatoes, cut into thin wedges

1 cup croutons

2 tablespoons finely shredded Parmesan cheese

Freshly ground black pepper

Start to finish: 25 minutes   Makes 4 servings

Cook pasta according to package directions; drain. Rinse with cold water; drain again.

Meanwhile, stir together salad dressing, lemon juice, and garlic; set aside.

In a large salad bowl combine pasta, romaine, and apple wedges. Pour dressing over salad; toss gently to coat. Sprinkle with croutons, Parmesan cheese, and pepper. Toss gently to combine.

Nutrition facts per serving: 381 cal., 16 g total fat (2 g sat. fat), 33 mg chol., 338 mg sodium, 47 g carbo., 3 g fiber, 14 g pro. Daily values: 24% vit. A, 42% vit. C, 15% calcium, 18% iron

pasta coleslaw

Coleslaw, our legacy from the early Dutch settlers (who called it *kool sla*), tastes newly minted with pasta, sweet mandarin oranges, and healthy shredded broccoli, available prepackaged as broccoli slaw.

Start to finish: 25 minutes   Makes 4 servings

Cook pasta according to package directions; drain. Rinse with cold water; drain again.

Meanwhile, for dressing, stir together mayonnaise, vinegar, mustard, sugar, and celery seed; set aside.

In a large bowl combine pasta, broccoli, kidney beans, and green onions. Pour dressing over pasta mixture; toss gently to coat. Stir in orange sections. Serve immediately or cover and chill for several hours.

Nutrition facts per serving: 395 cal., 15 g total fat (3 g sat. fat), 0 mg chol., 563 mg sodium, 58 g carbo., 8 g fiber, 12 g pro. Daily values: 5% vit. A, 54% vit. C, 52% calcium, 19% iron

4 ounces dried tiny bow ties
   (about 1½ cups)

⅔ cup light mayonnaise dressing
   or salad dressing

2 tablespoons white balsamic vinegar

1 tablespoon coarse-grain
   brown mustard

½ teaspoon sugar

½ teaspoon celery seed

3 cups packaged shredded broccoli
   (broccoli slaw mix)

1 15½-ounce can red kidney beans,
   rinsed and drained

¼ cup sliced green onions

1 11-ounce can mandarin orange
   sections, drained

hot soups,
cool tastes

soup with mixed pastas

Finally, the perfect use for all those leftover pastas that don't add up to a meal. And because your pantry stock is ever-changing, this soup is different every time.

Start to finish: 30 minutes   Makes 3 servings (5½ cups)

In a large saucepan bring chicken broth and water to boiling. Add bay leaves, onion, carrot, and garlic. Reduce heat and simmer, uncovered, for 10 minutes.

Meanwhile, rinse chicken; pat dry. Coarsely chop chicken. In a medium skillet heat oil over medium-high heat. Add chicken; cook and stir about 2 minutes or until browned.

Add chicken, desired pasta, and sage to saucepan. Simmer, uncovered, for 8 to 10 minutes or until the larger pieces of pasta are tender but firm. Remove bay leaves. Ladle soup into bowls.

Nutrition facts per serving: 220 cal., 6 g total fat (1 g sat. fat), 20 mg chol., 896 mg sodium, 28 g carbo., 2 g fiber, 14 g pro. Daily values: 79% vit. A, 8% vit. C, 3% calcium, 11% iron

4 cups reduced-sodium
chicken broth

1 cup water

3 bay leaves

1 large onion, chopped

1 large carrot, chopped

4 cloves garlic, minced

4 ounces skinless, boneless
chicken breasts

1 teaspoon olive oil or cooking oil

2 ounces various small pastas,
such as dried rotini, ditalini,
fusilli, wagon wheel
or shell macaroni, and/or
broken spaghetti

Snipped fresh sage

pasta & bean
chicken soup

Using canned white beans, canned tomatoes, cooked chicken, and purchased pesto moves dinner into the express lane. Try this trattoria tip: Place a slice of grilled bread in each bowl, then ladle the soup on top.

3½ cups reduced-sodium chicken broth

1 cup water

1 19-ounce can white kidney beans or great northern beans, rinsed and drained

2 cups chopped cooked chicken

1 14½-ounce can diced tomatoes with onion and garlic or diced tomatoes with basil, oregano, and garlic; undrained

1½ cups thinly sliced carrots

1 cup dried ditalini or tiny bow ties (4 ounces)

¼ cup pesto

Start to finish: 25 minutes Makes 5 servings (9 cups)

In a large saucepan combine chicken broth, water, beans, chicken, undrained tomatoes, carrots, and pasta.

Bring to boiling. Reduce heat and simmer, covered, about 10 minutes or until pasta is tender but firm. Stir in pesto. Ladle soup into bowls.

Nutrition facts per serving: 323 cal., 12 g total fat (1 g sat. fat), 46 mg chol., 914 mg sodium, 33 g carbo., 5 g fiber, 25 g pro. Daily values: 91% vit. A, 17% vit. C, 4% calcium, 15% iron

bean there, done that

Unlike most canned beans, dried beans that you cook yourself are preservative-free and virtually sodium-free. Make a big batch when you have some time, and freeze in recipe-size amounts (thaw before using). To cook 1 pound of dried beans: Rinse beans. Bring beans and 8 cups cold water to a boil, reduce heat, and simmer for 2 minutes. Remove from heat. Cover and let stand for 1 hour. Or, omit simmering and soak beans in cold water overnight in a covered pot. Drain and rinse. Fill the pot with beans and 8 cups fresh water. Bring to a boil, reduce heat, and simmer, covered, until tender (for at least 1 to 1½ hours).

indian chicken soup

In India cooks can spend a day at the market just selecting seasonings. Retaining all the vibrant flavor of Indian cuisine, but not its multitude of spices, this appealing, slightly exotic soup is done in less than 30 minutes.

Start to finish: 25 minutes   Makes 6 servings (8½ cups)

In a large saucepan melt margarine over medium heat. Add jalapeño pepper (if using), coriander, and cumin; cook for 1 minute. Add chicken broth, cilantro, and turmeric. Bring to boiling; add pasta. Return to boiling. Reduce heat and boil gently, uncovered, for 6 to 8 minutes or until pasta is nearly tender.

Stir in zucchini and tomato. Return to boiling. Reduce heat and boil gently, uncovered, about 2 minutes more or until pasta and zucchini are just tender. Stir in chicken; heat through. Ladle soup into bowls.

Nutrition facts per serving: 244 cal., 8 g total fat (1 g sat. fat), 45 mg chol., 712 mg sodium, 23 g carbo., 1 g fiber, 21 g pro. Daily values: 7% vit. A, 18% vit. C, 2% calcium, 14% iron

1	tablespoon margarine or butter
1	jalapeño pepper, seeded if desired, and finely chopped (optional)
1	teaspoon coriander seeds, crushed, or ½ teaspoon ground coriander
1	teaspoon cumin seeds, crushed, or ½ teaspoon ground cumin
6	cups chicken broth
2	tablespoons snipped fresh cilantro
½	teaspoon ground turmeric
1¼	cups dried small shell macaroni
2	cups sliced zucchini
1⅓	cups chopped tomato
2	cups chopped cooked chicken

crab & pasta gazpacho

Gazpacho—the chilled tomato-and-vegetable soup—was born in Spain but reinvented in California, where it's a summer menu favorite. This fast, fresh version full of sweet crab, juicy nectarines, and fragrant basil couldn't be from anywhere else.

Start to finish: 25 minutes   Makes 6 servings (8 cups)

Cook pasta according to package directions; drain. Rinse with cold water; drain again.

Meanwhile, in a large bowl stir together vegetable juice and lime juice. Stir in pasta, crabmeat, nectarines, tomatoes, cucumber, and basil. Ladle soup into bowls.

Nutrition facts per serving: 162 cal., 1 g total fat (0 g sat. fat), 28 mg chol., 947 mg sodium, 28 g carbo., 2 g fiber, 11 g pro. Daily values: 12% vit. A, 26% vit. C, 5% calcium, 16% iron

1 **cup dried small shell macaroni or bow ties (4 ounces)**

4 **cups hot-style vegetable juice, chilled**

1 **tablespoon lime juice or lemon juice**

6 **ounces cooked lump crabmeat, flaked, or chopped cooked chicken (about 1¼ cups)**

2 **medium nectarines, chopped (1⅓ cups)**

2 **plum tomatoes, chopped (¾ cup)**

¼ **cup chopped, seeded cucumber**

2 **tablespoons snipped fresh basil**

ravioli soup

No matter what's in season, this fast meal-in-a-bowl makes for year-round good eating. Always available refrigerated ravioli, cooked turkey sausage, and produce and pantry staples are why.

1 cup thinly sliced onion

1 clove garlic, minced

1 tablespoon margarine or butter

2¼ cups water

1 14½-ounce can reduced-sodium chicken broth or beef broth

1 9-ounce package refrigerated cheese-filled ravioli

4 ounces cooked smoked turkey sausage, halved lengthwise and thinly sliced (⅔ cup)

2 medium carrots, sliced (1 cup)

1 14½-ounce can low-sodium tomatoes, undrained and cut up

1 medium yellow summer squash or zucchini, halved lengthwise and sliced (1 cup)

4 teaspoons snipped fresh thyme or parsley

Start to finish: 25 minutes   Makes 4 servings (8 cups)

In a 4½-quart Dutch oven cook onion and garlic in margarine over medium-high heat for about 5 minutes or until golden brown, stirring frequently.

Carefully add water and broth. Bring to boiling. Add pasta, turkey sausage, and carrots. Return to boiling. Reduce the heat and simmer, uncovered, for 5 to 6 minutes or until pasta is tender but firm. Add tomatoes, yellow summer squash, and thyme; heat through. Ladle soup into bowls.

Nutrition facts per serving: 337 cal., 14 g total fat (6 g sat. fat), 74 mg chol., 871 mg sodium, 37 g carbo., 3 g fiber, 18 g pro. Daily values: 92% vit. A, 33% vit. C, 19% calcium, 19% iron

cabbage & pasta soup

Enjoy a reprieve from the daily grind. This hearty, German-style soup is conveniently created out of ready-cooked ham, frozen peas, and coleslaw mix, all in a prepared chicken broth.

Start to finish: 25 minutes   Makes 4 servings (6 cups)

In a large saucepan bring chicken broth, water, mustard, celery seed, and pepper to boiling (mixture may look curdled). Add pasta and ham; return to boiling.

Reduce heat and simmer, uncovered, for 10 to 12 minutes or until pasta is tender but firm. Stir in cabbage and peas; let stand for 5 minutes. Ladle soup into bowls.

Nutrition facts per serving: 203 cal., 4 g total fat (1 g sat. fat), 18 mg chol., 1,156 mg sodium, 27 g carbo., 3 g fiber, 15 g pro. Daily values: 41% vit. A, 64% vit. C, 4% calcium, 16% iron

4 cups reduced-sodium chicken broth

2 cups water

1 tablespoon German-style mustard
   or spicy brown mustard

½ teaspoon celery seed

¼ teaspoon coarsely ground pepper

1¼ cups dried radiatore or medium
   shell macaroni

1 cup chopped cooked ham

3 cups packaged shredded cabbage
   with carrot (coleslaw mix)

1 cup frozen peas

chinese beef & noodle soup

Stir-fry is a uniquely Chinese invention, but cooks everywhere use it for its quick-to-the-table qualities. A peppery steak-and-ginger duo turns pasta soup into a hearty meal.

3¾ cups water

2 14½-ounce cans beef broth (3½ cups)

3 tablespoons reduced-sodium soy sauce

1 teaspoon sesame oil

1½ cups dried gemelli (6 ounces)

8 ounces beef flank steak

4 teaspoons cooking oil

1 to 2 tablespoons grated gingerroot

6 cloves garlic, minced

½ cup sliced green onions

½ to 1 teaspoon crushed red pepper

5 cups coarsely shredded bok choy

Start to finish: 25 minutes   Makes 6 servings (9 cups)

In a large saucepan combine water, beef broth, soy sauce, and sesame oil. Bring to boiling. Add pasta. Return to boiling. Reduce heat and boil gently for 10 to 12 minutes or until pasta is tender but firm.

Meanwhile, thinly slice steak across the grain into thin, bite-size strips. Pour cooking oil into a wok or large skillet. Preheat over medium-high heat. Stir-fry gingerroot and garlic for 15 seconds. Add the beef, green onions, and crushed red pepper. Stir-fry for 2 to 3 minutes or until desired doneness. Remove meat mixture from wok; add to saucepan along with bok choy. Heat through. Ladle soup into bowls.

Nutrition facts per serving: 229 cal., 7 g total fat (2 g sat. fat), 18 mg chol., 746 mg sodium, 26 g carbo., 1 g fiber, 14 g pro. Daily values: 10% vit. A, 20% vit. C, 6% calcium, 16% iron

stock tips

Homemade stock tastes best, but prepared broth is handy when time is short. Use canned chicken, beef, or vegetable broth right from the can (if condensed, dilute as directed on the label). Or, opt for instant bouillon granules or cubes: For 1 cup of broth, mix 1 cup water with 1 teaspoon granules or 1 cube.

meatball soup

Gear up for a delicious soup supper that quick-cooks with assembly-line efficiency. The meatballs can be shaped, baked, and frozen up to three months ahead, leaving little to do at the last minute.

73

Start to finish: 30 minutes   Makes 4 servings (6 cups)

In a medium mixing bowl combine egg white, bread crumbs, Parmesan cheese, onion, the ¼ teaspoon Italian seasoning, and pepper. Add ground beef; mix well. Shape meat mixture into 36 balls; place in a large shallow baking pan. Bake in a 350° oven about 15 minutes or until no pink remains. Drain off fat.*

Meanwhile, in a large saucepan stir together beef broth, undrained tomatoes, water, and the ½ teaspoon Italian seasoning. Bring to boiling; add pasta and frozen vegetables. Return to boiling. Reduce heat and simmer, covered, about 10 minutes or until pasta and vegetables are tender. Add meatballs; heat through. Ladle soup into bowls.

Nutrition facts per serving: 243 cal., 7 g total fat (3 g sat. fat), 39 mg chol., 902 mg sodium, 26 g carbo., 1 g fiber, 18 g pro. Daily values: 22% vit. A, 27% vit. C, 8% calcium, 16% iron

*Note: Cooked meatballs may be frozen for up to three months. Thaw in the refrigerator before using.

- 1 slightly beaten egg white
- ½ cup soft bread crumbs (¾ slice)
- 2 tablespoons grated Parmesan cheese
- 2 tablespoons finely chopped onion
- ¼ teaspoon Italian seasoning, crushed
- ⅛ teaspoon pepper
- ½ pound lean ground beef
- 1 14½-ounce can beef broth
- 1 14½-ounce can diced tomatoes with onion and garlic, undrained
- 1½ cups water
- ½ teaspoon Italian seasoning, crushed
- ½ cup small dried pasta such as tripolini, ditalini, stellini, or orzo
- 1 cup loose-pack frozen mixed vegetables

spring green pasta soup

Thin strips of cooked egg, exquisite spring vegetables, and wispy threads of angel hair pasta compose a delicate soup with the airy lightness of a heavenly omelet.

Start to finish: 30 minutes   Makes 4 servings (6½ cups)

In a large saucepan bring chicken broth and water to boiling.

Meanwhile, in a medium skillet cook eggs in oil over medium heat, without stirring, for 2 to 3 minutes or until eggs are set. To remove cooked eggs, loosen edges and invert skillet over a cutting board; cut eggs into thin, bite-size strips. Set aside.

Add pasta, leeks, and garlic to chicken broth. Boil gently, uncovered, about 3 minutes or until pasta is nearly tender. Add sugar snap peas, asparagus, dill, and lemon peel. Return to boiling. Boil gently about 2 minutes more or until vegetables are crisp-tender; stir in egg strips. Ladle soup into bowls.

Nutrition facts per serving: 235 cal., 7 g total fat (1 g sat. fat), 107 mg chol., 684 mg sodium, 33 g carbo., 4 g fiber, 12 g pro. Daily values: 8% vit. A, 46% vit. C, 5% calcium, 19% iron

- **4 cups reduced-sodium chicken broth**
- **2 cups water**
- **2 slightly beaten eggs**
- **2 teaspoons cooking oil**
- **4 ounces dried angel hair pasta, broken into 2-inch pieces**
- **2 medium leeks, sliced, or ⅔ cup sliced green onions**
- **2 cloves garlic, minced**
- **4 ounces sugar snap peas, cut in half crosswise (about 1 cup)**
- **8 ounces asparagus, cut into 1-inch pieces (about 1 cup)**
- **2 tablespoons snipped fresh dill**
- **2 teaspoons finely shredded lemon peel**

creamy carrot & pasta soup

Do you hear the reggae rhythms? Or is it just the hot Jamaican spices in this creamy pasta soup that dance in your mouth? It's a tropical trip via a dash of jerk seasoning—a unique island blend of spices, herbs, and fiery chilies that is Jamaica's own.

2 14½-ounce cans chicken broth (3½ cups)

2 cups sliced carrots

1 large potato, peeled and diced

1 cup chopped onion

1 tablespoon grated gingerroot

½ to 1 teaspoon Jamaican jerk seasoning

8 ounces dried tricolor radiatore or rotini

1½ cups milk or one 12-ounce can evaporated skim milk

Snipped fresh chives (optional)

Start to finish: 30 minutes   Makes 4 servings (7 cups)

In a large saucepan combine chicken broth, carrots, potato, onion, gingerroot, and Jamaican jerk seasoning. Bring to boiling. Reduce heat and simmer, covered, for 15 to 20 minutes or until vegetables are very tender. Cool slightly.

Meanwhile, cook pasta according to package directions; drain.

Place one-fourth of the vegetable mixture in a food processor. Cover and process until smooth. Process remaining vegetable mixture one-fourth at a time. Return all to saucepan. Stir in pasta and milk; heat through. Ladle soup into bowls. If desired, sprinkle with chives.

Nutrition facts per serving: 363 cal., 4 g total fat (2 g sat. fat), 8 mg chol., 750 mg sodium, 65 g carbo., 3 g fiber, 16 g pro. Daily values: 91% vit. A, 10% vit. C, 12% calcium, 20% iron

vermicelli & onion soup

Rustic onion soup takes brasserie chefs hours to prepare, but here it's made easy with a simple, sherry-garnished broth ready in a fraction of the time. Accompany it with a salad of frizzy green chicory, and voilà, dinner chez vous.

2 ounces dried vermicelli, broken into 2-inch pieces (½ cup)

1 tablespoon olive oil or cooking oil

2 medium onions, thinly sliced

2 14½-ounce cans beef broth (3½ cups)

½ cup water

2 tablespoons dry sherry

Dash ground red pepper

2 medium tomatoes, chopped (1½ cups)

4 slices French bread

½ cup shredded Swiss cheese

Start to finish: 35 minutes Makes 4 servings (5 cups)

In a large saucepan cook the uncooked pasta over medium-low heat in hot oil until golden brown, stirring frequently. Remove pasta with a slotted spoon; drain on paper towels. Set aside.

Add sliced onions to oil in saucepan. Cook, covered, about 10 minutes or until onions are very tender, stirring occasionally. (If necessary, add more oil to saucepan during cooking.) Stir in beef broth, water, sherry, and red pepper. Bring mixture to boiling. Stir in pasta. Reduce heat and simmer, covered, about 10 minutes or until pasta is tender but still firm. Stir in tomatoes; heat through.

Meanwhile, toast both sides of bread under the broiler. Sprinkle cheese over bread. Place under broiler about 1 minute or until cheese melts and turns light brown.

To serve, ladle soup into bowls. Float bread atop.

Nutrition facts per serving: 259 cal., 9 g total fat (3 g sat. fat), 13 mg chol., 866 mg sodium, 31 g carbo., 1 g fiber, 11 g pro. Daily values: 7% vit. A, 22% vit. C, 15% calcium, 13% iron

vegetable minestrone

Italians fortify their chunky vegetable soups with everything from rice to beans to potatoes to pasta, depending on the region. Southern Italian cooks would call this version—packed with bits of spaghetti—their own.

Start to finish: 35 minutes   Makes 4 servings (7 cups)

In a large saucepan cook onion, carrot, and garlic in hot oil until tender. Stir in water, tomatoes, chicken broth, basil, sage, and pepper.

Bring to boiling. Reduce heat and simmer, covered, for 10 minutes. Add succotash. Return to boiling; stir in pasta. Reduce heat and simmer, covered, about 10 minutes or until pasta is tender but firm. Stir in the zucchini.

Ladle into soup bowls. Sprinkle with Parmesan cheese.

Nutrition facts per serving: 271 cal., 6 g total fat (1 g sat. fat), 2 mg chol., 390 mg sodium, 47 g carbo., 10 g fiber, 11 g pro. Daily values: 51% vit. A, 57% vit. C, 7% calcium, 19% iron

- 1 cup chopped onion
- ½ cup chopped carrot
- 1 clove garlic, minced
- 1 tablespoon olive oil or cooking oil
- 2 cups water
- 2 cups chopped peeled tomatoes or one 16-ounce can tomatoes, undrained and cut up
- 1 14½-ounce can reduced-sodium chicken broth
- 1 teaspoon dried basil, crushed
- ⅛ teaspoon ground sage
- ⅛ teaspoon pepper
- 1 10-ounce package frozen succotash
- 2 ounces dried spaghetti, broken into bite-size pieces (about ½ cup)
- 1 cup thinly sliced zucchini
- 2 tablespoons grated Parmesan cheese

new takes on noodles

chicken, long beans, & tomato stir-fry

If you think good taste is hard to measure, consider Chinese long beans. A star of Asian stir-fries, these dark green, pencil-thin legumes average 1½ feet of meaty, crunchy flavor. Many supermarket produce sections now stock them.

Start to finish: 30 minutes   Makes 4 servings

Cook rice noodles in boiling, lightly salted water for 3 to 5 minutes or until tender. Or, cook egg noodles according to package directions. Drain noodles; keep warm.

Meanwhile, in a large skillet heat 2 teaspoons of the oil. Add garlic and stir-fry for 15 seconds. Add beans; stir-fry for 2 minutes. Carefully add water to skillet. Reduce heat to low; cover and simmer for 6 to 8 minutes or until beans are crisp-tender. Remove beans from skillet.

Toss chicken with Cajun seasoning. Add the remaining 2 teaspoons cooking oil to skillet. Add chicken; stir-fry for 3 to 4 minutes or until no longer pink. Add beans, tomatoes, and vinegar; heat through. Serve over noodles.

Nutrition facts per serving: 361 cal., 5 g total fat (1 g sat. fat), 45 mg chol., 334 mg sodium, 54 g carbo., 5 g fiber, 25 g pro. Daily values: 13% vit. A, 38% vit. C, 6% calcium, 21% iron

- 6 ounces wide rice noodles or dried egg noodles
- 4 teaspoons cooking oil
- 2 cloves garlic, minced
- 1 pound Chinese long beans or whole green beans, cut into 3-inch pieces
- ¼ cup water
- 12 ounces skinless, boneless chicken breast halves, cut into strips
- 1 teaspoon Cajun seasoning or other spicy seasoning blend
- 2 medium tomatoes, cut into thin wedges
- 2 tablespoons raspberry vinegar

ratatouille
over **egg** noodles

Familiar on dinner tables from Provence to Paris, this chunky, aromatic mélange of eggplant, tomatoes, herbs, and garlic is a bistro classic, streamlined here for busy lives.

½ **pound ground raw chicken**

1 **tablespoon cooking oil**

1 **large eggplant, cubed (5 cups)**

2 **onions, cut into wedges**

2 **medium green sweet peppers, cut into strips**

2 **cloves garlic, minced**

1 **15-ounce can tomato sauce**

1 **14½-ounce can diced tomatoes, undrained**

2 **teaspoons dried marjoram, crushed**

¼ **teaspoon ground red pepper**

8 **ounces dried wide egg noodles**

Start to finish: 35 minutes   Makes 4 servings

For sauce, in a 4½-quart Dutch oven cook chicken in hot oil until just browned. Add eggplant, onions, sweet pepper strips, and garlic. Cook about 3 minutes or until vegetables are crisp-tender, stirring mixture occasionally.

Add tomato sauce, undrained tomatoes, marjoram, and ground red pepper. Bring mixture just to boiling. Reduce heat and simmer, uncovered, for 15 minutes, stirring occasionally.

Meanwhile, cook noodles according to package directions; drain. Transfer noodles to a warm serving dish. Spoon sauce over noodles. Serve immediately.

Nutrition facts per serving: 403 cal., 9 g total fat (2 g sat. fat), 76 mg chol., 948 mg sodium, 63 g carbo., 8 g fiber, 19 g pro. Daily values: 22% vit. A, 104% vit. C, 7% calcium, 36% iron

the **daily** grind
You can now find ground raw chicken at most grocery meat counters, but it's hard to tell at a glance whether it's breast meat, dark meat, or both. To be sure you get what you want (strictly breast meat without the skin is the leanest choice), ask the butcher to grind it fresh for you. Or, do it yourself: Boneless chicken breasts grind up in seconds in a food processor.

sesame beef

Get a jump on dinner. Slice the vegetables and beef ahead and refrigerate airtight. Minutes before mealtime, swirl them in a wok or skillet and serve up swiftly with Chinese rice noodles.

Start to finish: 30 minutes   Makes 4 servings

Cook rice noodles in boiling, lightly salted water for 3 to 5 minutes or just until tender. Or, cook egg noodles according to package directions. Drain noodles; keep warm.

Meanwhile, pour 1 tablespoon of the oil into a wok or large skillet. Preheat over medium-high heat. Stir-fry carrots in hot oil for 2 minutes. Add celery and sweet pepper. Stir-fry 1 to 2 minutes more or until vegetables are crisp-tender. Remove vegetables from wok.

Add remaining oil to hot wok. Stir-fry beef for 2 minutes. Sprinkle sesame seed over beef; continue to stir-fry about 1 minute more or until beef is of desired doneness. Return vegetables to wok; add stir-fry sauce. Cook and stir for 1 to 2 minutes or until hot. Serve over noodles.

Nutrition facts per serving: 419 cal., 16 g total fat (4 g sat. fat), 57 mg chol., 590 mg sodium, 47 g carbo., 2 g fiber, 22 g pro. Daily values: 94% vit. A, 56% vit. C, 3% calcium, 4% iron

- **6 ounces wide rice noodles or dried egg noodles**
- **2 tablespoons cooking oil or peanut oil**
- **2 medium carrots, thinly sliced (1 cup)**
- **2 stalks celery, cut into thin, bite-size strips**
- **1 red sweet pepper, cut into thin, bite-size strips**
- **12 ounces boneless beef sirloin steak or beef top round steak, cut into bite-size strips**
- **1 tablespoon sesame seed**
- **⅓ cup bottled stir-fry sauce**

asian beef & noodle bowl

Already fast to toss together, this satisfying Asian noodle supper zooms to conclusion if you stop first at the grocery salad bar and pick up prewashed spinach, shredded carrots, and a jar each of minced ginger and garlic.

85

Start to finish: 30 minutes   Makes 4 servings

In a large saucepan bring water to boiling. If desired, break up noodles; drop noodles into the boiling water. (Do not use the flavor packets.) Return to boiling; boil for 2 to 3 minutes or just until noodles are tender but firm, stirring occasionally. Drain noodles.

Pour oil into a wok or large skillet. Preheat over medium-high heat. Stir-fry beef, gingerroot, and garlic in hot oil for 2 to 3 minutes or to desired doneness. Push beef from the center of the wok. Add beef broth and soy sauce. Bring to boiling. Reduce heat and stir meat into broth mixture. Cook and stir 1 to 2 minutes more or until heated through.

Add noodles, spinach, carrots, and mint to mixture in wok; toss to combine. Ladle mixture into soup bowls. If desired, sprinkle with peanuts.

Nutrition facts per serving: 211 cal., 10 g total fat (3 g sat. fat), 47 mg chol., 690 mg sodium, 11 g carbo., 2 g fiber, 20 g pro. Daily values: 101% vit. A, 23% vit. C, 4% calcium, 26% iron

Note: If using cooking oil, stir ⅛ to ¼ teaspoon ground red pepper into oil.

4   cups water

2   3-ounce packages ramen noodles

2   teaspoons chili oil or cooking oil*

12 ounces beef flank steak or beef
     top round steak, cut into
     bite-size strips

1   teaspoon grated gingerroot

2   cloves garlic, minced

1   cup beef broth

1   tablespoon soy sauce

2   cups torn fresh spinach

1   cup shredded carrots

¼   cup snipped fresh mint or cilantro

¼   cup chopped peanuts (optional)

broccoli, prosciutto, & noodles

An Italian opera about prosciutto? Far-fetched, but the Italians do rhapsodize about their sweet, rosy, salt-cured ham, a traditional specialty of Parma. Just a little makes a simple, chunky pasta sauce sing with authentic Italian country flavor.

- 4 ounces dried medium egg noodles (2 cups)

- 2 tablespoons olive oil

- 2 cloves garlic, minced

- 2 cups broccoli flowerets

- 1 medium red onion, cut into thin wedges

- 1 cup chopped, thinly sliced prosciutto or cubed cooked ham

- ¼ cup oil-packed dried tomatoes, drained and slivered

- ¾ cup reduced-sodium chicken broth

- 2 tablespoons snipped fresh oregano

  Pepper (optional)

Start to finish: 25 minutes   Makes 4 servings

Cook noodles according to package directions; drain.

Meanwhile, pour olive oil into a wok or large skillet. (Add more oil as necessary during cooking.) Preheat over medium-high heat. Stir-fry garlic in hot oil for 15 seconds. Add broccoli and onion; stir-fry about 6 minutes or until crisp-tender. Add prosciutto and dried tomatoes; stir-fry 1 minute more.

Carefully pour in chicken broth; add oregano. Bring to boiling; add noodles. Cook and stir about 1 minute more or until heated through. If desired, season with pepper.

Nutrition facts per serving: 288 cal., 16 g total fat (1 g sat. fat), 24 mg chol., 656 mg sodium, 24 g carbo., 2 g fiber, 13 g pro. Daily values: 7% vit. A, 66% vit. C, 3% calcium, 10% iron

glass noodles with
tenderloin & broccoli rabe

Bite-size bits of quick-cooked pork tenderloin and broccoli rabe—a dark green, leafy vegetable that looks like broccoli, but has a little more bite—float on transparent, threadlike Chinese pasta. The noodles appear delicate, but are actually nice and chewy.

Start to finish: 30 minutes   Makes 4 servings

Soak noodles in hot water for 10 minutes; drain. Rinse in cold water; drain well. Use scissors to cut noodles into desired length. Cook noodles in boiling water for 3 minutes; drain. Keep warm.

Meanwhile, trim fat from pork. Thinly slice pork across the grain into bite-size strips.

Pour 1 tablespoon of the oil into a wok or large skillet. Preheat over medium-high heat. Stir-fry mushrooms and onion for 3 to 4 minutes or until onion is just tender. Add broccoli rabe; cover and cook about 4 minutes or until crisp-tender, stirring once. Remove vegetables from wok; set aside.

Add remaining oil to wok. Stir-fry pork for 2 to 3 minutes or until no pink remains. Push pork from center of wok. Add stir-fry sauce and crushed red pepper to center of wok. Stir in vegetables and pork. Cook and stir for 1 to 2 minutes or until hot. Serve over noodles.

Nutrition facts per serving: 350 cal., 11 g total fat (2 g sat. fat), 61 mg chol., 711 mg sodium, 37 g carbo., 3 g fiber, 27 g pro. Daily values: 8% vit. A, 73% vit. C, 44% calcium, 16% iron

- 4 ounces cellophane noodles
- ¾ pound pork tenderloin or lean boneless pork
- 2 tablespoons cooking oil
- 1½ cups sliced fresh mushrooms
- 1 medium onion, cut into wedges
- 8 ounces broccoli rabe, cut into 1-inch pieces (6 cups), or 3 cups broccoli flowerets
- ⅓ cup bottled stir-fry sauce
- ¼ teaspoon crushed red pepper

party pancit

Expand your social calendar to busy weeknights with this easy stir-fry that's sure to be the life of any dinner party. Pancit canton is both a dried egg noodle and the name of the Filipino version of Chinese chow mein.

89

Start to finish: 30 minutes   Makes 4 servings

Pour oil into a 12-inch skillet. Preheat over medium-high heat. Stir-fry onion, gingerroot, and garlic for 1 minute. Carefully add chicken broth, water, and soy sauce to skillet. Bring to boiling. Stir in mushrooms, asparagus, carrots, and noodles. Return to boiling. Reduce heat to medium and cook for 4 minutes.

Add shrimp to skillet. Cook for 3 to 4 minutes more or until shrimp are opaque, noodles are tender, and most of the liquid is absorbed. Serve immediately.

Nutrition facts per serving: 353 cal., 7 g total fat (1 g sat. fat), 180 mg chol., 740 mg sodium, 47 g carbo., 4 g fiber, 25 g pro. Daily values: 90% vit. A, 31% vit. C, 6% calcium, 37% iron

1   **tablespoon cooking oil**

½   **cup chopped onion**

2   **teaspoons grated gingerroot**

2   **cloves garlic, minced**

1   **14½-ounce can reduced-sodium chicken broth**

1   **cup water**

2   **tablespoons reduced-sodium soy sauce**

1½   **cups sliced fresh shiitake mushrooms or cremini mushrooms**

¾   **pound asparagus, cut into 1-inch pieces**

1   **cup thinly bias-sliced carrots**

8   **ounces pancit canton noodles or dried spaghetti, broken**

12   **ounces peeled and deveined shrimp, cut lengthwise in half (leave tails intact, if desired)**

vegetarian noodles

With plump, delicious beans, the best vegetables ever, and a dose of good Parmesan cheese, this engaging pasta main course is a real crowd-pleaser. Even dedicated meat-eaters will clean their plates!

90

6 ounces dried somen noodles or
  dried angel hair pasta

3 small zucchini, halved lengthwise
  and cut into ¼-inch slices
  (3 cups)

2 cloves garlic, minced

1 tablespoon olive oil

3 cups chopped plum tomatoes
  or two 14½-ounce cans diced
  tomatoes, drained

2 tablespoons snipped fresh basil

¼ teaspoon salt

1 15-ounce can black beans or white
  kidney beans, rinsed and drained

¼ cup shredded Parmesan cheese
  (optional)

Start to finish: 25 minutes   Makes 4 servings

Cook noodles according to package directions; drain.

Meanwhile, in a large skillet cook and stir zucchini and garlic in hot oil for 3 to 4 minutes until zucchini is tender. Add tomatoes, basil, and salt; cook and stir for 2 minutes more.

Add beans; heat through. Add noodles; toss gently to combine. Transfer to a warm serving dish. If desired, sprinkle with Parmesan cheese.

Nutrition facts per serving: 301 cal., 5 g total fat (1 g sat. fat), 0 mg chol., 1,196 mg sodium, 58 g carbo., 9 g fiber, 14 g pro. Daily values: 12% vit. A, 60% vit. C, 5% calcium, 18% iron

use your **noodle**

Made from wheat flour, dried Japanese somen noodles are very fine (similar to Italian angel hair pasta) and most often white. You'll find them, wrapped in bundles, where Asian foods are sold, in such variations as plain, green tea (cha somen), egg yolk (tomago somen), or plum (ume somen).

buckwheat noodle stir-fry

Brownish, speckled soba noodles from Japan are favorites in that country's north where the nutty flavor of buckwheat is preferred. Softer udon noodles, using wheat, are more popular in the south.

Start to finish: 30 minutes   Makes 4 servings

Cook buckwheat noodles or spaghetti according to package directions. Drain; keep warm.

Rinse turkey breast tenderloin; pat dry. Cut turkey into thin, bite-size strips; set aside.

Pour cooking oil into a wok or large skillet. (Add more oil as necessary during cooking.) Preheat over medium-high heat. Stir-fry peas and sweet pepper for 2 minutes. Add green onions. Stir-fry 1 to 2 minutes more or until vegetables are crisp-tender. Remove vegetables from wok.

Add turkey and sesame oil to the hot wok. Stir-fry for 3 to 4 minutes or until no longer pink. Add plum sauce and crushed red pepper. Stir in vegetables; heat through. Serve over noodles.

Nutrition facts per serving: 331 cal., 6 g total fat (1 g sat. fat), 37 mg chol., 384 mg sodium, 48 g carbo., 3 g fiber, 25 g pro. Daily values: 18% vit. A, 110% vit. C, 4% calcium, 22% iron

6 ounces dried soba (buckwheat) noodles or whole wheat spaghetti

12 ounces turkey breast tenderloin

2 teaspoons cooking oil

2 cups sugar snap peas

1 medium red sweet pepper, cut into thin strips

4 green onions, bias-sliced into 1-inch pieces

1 teaspoon toasted sesame oil

½ cup bottled plum sauce

¼ teaspoon crushed red pepper

spaetzle with caramelized onions

In every Swiss kitchen you'll find a spaetzle maker, a type of sieve cooks use to shape these tiny dumplings. Dried spaetzle, available at most markets, saves all the old-country flavor—and you many steps.

Start to finish: 30 minutes   Makes 4 servings

In a large skillet cook onions, covered, in hot margarine over medium-low heat for 13 to 15 minutes or until onions are tender. Uncover; add sweet pepper strips, brown sugar, and vinegar. Cook and stir over medium-high heat for 4 to 5 minutes or until onions are golden. Stir in the chicken broth, half-and-half, dill, and pepper. Boil gently until mixture is thickened.

Meanwhile, cook spaetzle according to package directions, adding Brussels sprouts to the water with the spaetzle. Drain; return to saucepan. Add caramelized onion mixture and pork to saucepan. Cook and stir over low heat until spaetzle are well-coated and mixture is heated through. Transfer to a warm serving dish.

Nutrition facts per serving: 374 cal., 15 g total fat (5 g sat. fat), 91 mg chol., 279 mg sodium, 42 g carbo., 5 g fiber, 20 g pro. Daily values: 19% vit. A, 162% vit. C, 9% calcium, 20% iron

- 2 **large onions, cut into thin wedges (2 cups)**
- 2 **tablespoons margarine or butter**
- 1 **medium yellow, orange, or red sweet pepper, cut into bite-size strips**
- 4 **teaspoons brown sugar**
- 1 **tablespoon cider vinegar**
- ⅓ **cup chicken broth**
- ⅓ **cup half-and-half or light cream**
- 1 **tablespoon snipped fresh dill**
- ⅛ **teaspoon pepper**
- 4 **ounces dried spaetzle or kluski-style egg noodles**
- 2 **cups halved Brussels sprouts**
- 1 **cup cooked lean boneless pork or ham, cut into bite-size strips**

By making a few conversions, cooks in Australia, Canada, and the United Kingdom can use the recipes in *Better Homes and Gardens® Fresh and Simple™ Pasta Pronto* with confidence. The charts on this page provide a guide for converting measurements from the U.S. customary system, which is used throughout this book, to the imperial and metric systems. There also is a conversion table for oven temperatures to accommodate the differences in oven calibrations.

Product Differences: Most of the ingredients called for in the recipes in this book are available in English-speaking countries. However, some are known by different names. Here are some common American ingredients and their possible counterparts:

- Sugar is granulated or castor sugar.
- Powdered sugar is icing sugar.
- All-purpose flour is plain household flour or white flour. When self-rising flour is used in place of all-purpose flour in a recipe that calls for leavening, omit the leavening agent (baking soda or baking powder) and salt.
- Light-colored corn syrup is golden syrup.
- Cornstarch is cornflour.
- Baking soda is bicarbonate of soda.
- Vanilla is vanilla essence.
- Green, red, or yellow sweet peppers are capsicums.
- Golden raisins are sultanas.

Volume and Weight: Americans traditionally use cup measures for liquid and solid ingredients. The chart, above right, shows the approximate imperial and metric equivalents. If you are accustomed to weighing solid ingredients, the following approximate equivalents will be helpful.

- 1 cup butter, castor sugar, or rice = 8 ounces = about 250 grams
- 1 cup flour = 4 ounces = about 125 grams
- 1 cup icing sugar = 5 ounces = about 150 grams

Spoon measures are used for smaller amounts of ingredients. Although the size of the tablespoon varies slightly in different countries, for practical purposes and for recipes in this book, a straight substitution is all that's necessary.

Measurements made using cups or spoons always should be level unless stated otherwise.

Equivalents: U.S. = Australia/U.K.

⅛ teaspoon = 0.5 ml
¼ teaspoon = 1 ml
½ teaspoon = 2 ml
1 teaspoon = 5 ml
1 tablespoon = 1 tablespoon
¼ cup = 2 tablespoons = 2 fluid ounces = 60 ml
⅓ cup = ¼ cup = 3 fluid ounces = 90 ml
½ cup = ⅓ cup = 4 fluid ounces = 120 ml
⅔ cup = ½ cup = 5 fluid ounces = 150 ml
¾ cup = ⅔ cup = 6 fluid ounces = 180 ml
1 cup = ¾ cup = 8 fluid ounces = 240 ml
1¼ cups = 1 cup
2 cups = 1 pint
1 quart = 1 liter
½ inch = 1.27 cm
1 inch = 2.54 cm

Baking Pan Sizes

American	Metric
8×1½-inch round baking pan	20×4-cm cake tin
9×1½-inch round baking pan	23×3.5-cm cake tin
11×7×1½-inch baking pan	28×18×4-cm baking tin
13×9×2-inch baking pan	30×20×3-cm baking tin
2-quart rectangular baking dish	30×20×3-cm baking tin
15×10×1-inch baking pan	30×25×2-cm baking tin (Swiss roll tin)
9-inch pie plate	22×4- or 23×4-cm pie plate
7- or 8-inch springform pan	18- or 20-cm springform or loose-bottom cake tin
9×5×3-inch loaf pan	23×13×7-cm or 2-pound narrow loaf tin or pâté tin
1½-quart casserole	1.5-liter casserole
2-quart casserole	2-liter casserole

Oven Temperature Equivalents

Fahrenheit Setting	Celsius Setting*	Gas Setting
300°F	150°C	Gas Mark 2 (slow)
325°F	160°C	Gas Mark 3 (moderately slow)
350°F	180°C	Gas Mark 4 (moderate)
375°F	190°C	Gas Mark 5 (moderately hot)
400°F	200°C	Gas Mark 6 (hot)
425°F	220°C	Gas Mark 7
450°F	230°C	Gas Mark 8 (very hot)
Broil		Grill

Electric and gas ovens may be calibrated using Celsius. However, for an electric oven, increase the Celsius setting 10 to 20 degrees when cooking above 160°C. For convection or forced-air ovens (gas or electric), lower the temperature setting 10°C when cooking at all heat levels.